TOO CLOSE
FOR
COMFORT

First published in 2015 by
Blacker Limited

1 2 3 4 5 6 7 8 9 10

Text © Eric Brown 2015
Paintings © Michael Turner 2015
www.studio88.co.uk

A CIP catalogue record for this book is
available from the British Library.

ISBN 978-1-897739-96-9

Printed in China on behalf of
Latitude Press

Blacker Limited
Hillcroft Barn
Coombe Hill Road
East Grinstead
West Sussex
RH19 4LY

E: info@blackerdesign.co.uk
W: www.blackerdesign.co.uk

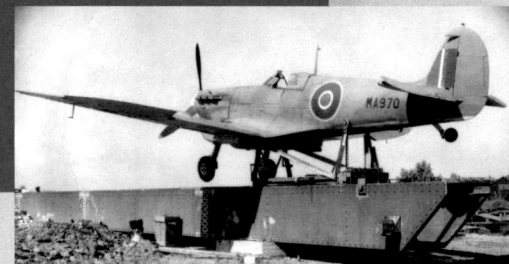

TOO CLOSE FOR COMFORT

ONE MAN'S CLOSE ENCOUNTERS
OF THE TERMINAL KIND

CAPTAIN ERIC 'WINKLE' BROWN
CBE DSC AFC RN

WITH ORIGINAL PAINTINGS BY
MICHAEL TURNER
FGAvA

BLACKER LIMITED

Contents

Foreword

By Eric Brown

Test flying, particularly before the days of simulation, computerisation and ejection seats, was a dangerous profession, but was accepted as such by those lucky enough to be involved.

It was a small community, and I first met Neil Armstrong at RAE, Bedford in 1971, some two years after his historic lunar landing, and we instantly became firm friends. Since we were both naval test pilots, our conversations revolved around flying and inevitably we compared our test flying careers. They had followed very similar paths, both having been involved in combat from carriers, high speed and transonic flight testing and rocketry. During one conversation, he remarked that my ratio of near misses to test hours flown was unusually high and that he wanted to analyse the reasons. As an outcome of that meeting Neil produced a list of my close encounters, and these form the narrative of this book.

Many of these exploits have been mentioned in previous books, but there are a few which have not been aired in public.

The Seafire Forth Bridge episode (opposite) being one of them. The reason this remained secret for close on 60 years was that at the time, had I been caught, I would have been in deep trouble. As it was, someone did ring the local RAF base to tell them that a Spitfire had looped each span of the bridge, assuming it was one of their pilots. The RAF crews all denied any responsibility, but were still reprimanded by their CO.

In my defence, the Forth Bridge is an amazing landmark and proved too much of a temptation for many young fighter pilots. In 1941 when 802 Squadron had just taken delivery of their new Grumman Wildcats from America, a group of us made a habit of flying under the bridge on our return from training flights. Eventually word got out and a daily crowd began to form. Far from reporting us, the local police regarded the spectacle as more of a morale booster for the local population and restricted their efforts to simply marshalling the crowd.

Before I had any thought of going into print, another friend, Michael Turner, President of the Guild of Aviation Artists heard of the list and felt the content would present an appealing challenge to illustrate. We discussed this and here is the end result, with just one major exception, a near fatal incident in the DH 108. This occurred when it developed a runaway longitudinal oscillation at a high Mach number. A pilot flying alongside described what he saw as the blur of an unidentifiable machine – hardly an objet d'art.

There can be no doubt that Michael's paintings perfectly capture the excitement and drama of each incident, putting the reader very much in the hot seat.

The infamous de Havilland
DH 108 VW120, which very
nearly did for me!

Foreword

By Michael Turner

Having had the pleasure of knowing Eric for some years, it had been in my mind that his extraordinary life and numerous exploits and adventures as a pilot would be wonderful to record in paintings, particularly as there was never a camera on the spot on countless occasions of instant and unexpected activity.

When Brian M Service told me about a particular episode involving Eric looping the spans of the Forth Bridge in a Seafire, which had caught his imagination to such an extent that he asked me to capture the event in a painting, I was very excited at the prospect of at least tackling one of his many adventures. Eric's clear recall of the event was inspirational, and, having completed the Forth Bridge painting, the idea of a book of selected incidents was re-kindled. When I suggested this to Eric, he was very enthusiastic, and approached his publishers, Blacker Design, for a reaction.

To my delight, they were most positive, and the project was under way. Eric came up with a short list of fifteen episodes which came under the heading of 'Too Close for Comfort'. Guided by his own vivid and amazingly clear descriptions, I set about capturing each one in a visual interpretation of the circumstances, all of which had to gain the approval of the man who was there at the time in the hot seat. I had many fascinating discussions with Eric as we fine tuned the details of each event.

I realise that these paintings only scratch the surface of an exceptional life at the cutting edge of flying, not only in combat in the Second World War, but as a test pilot who explored many unknown boundaries and survived. I feel very privileged to have had this opportunity to show my deep respect for such an amazing and unassuming man.

An unexpected mission

A nail-biting sortie –
the result of volunteering

12 April 1941

An unexpected mission

A nail-biting sortie – the result of volunteering

In late 1939, as I joined the Fleet Air Arm, I found a kindred spirit in young Graham Fletcher, who came from a medical family of doctors. We had both joined up as soon as war broke out, he had come straight from St Paul's School, having spent his schoolboy savings on learning to fly, and I was just down from Edinburgh University.

We did our naval flying training together at Netheravon and Yeovilton, where we were introduced to the Blackburn Skua and taught the elements of dive-bombing.

In 1941 we were both posted to No. 802 Squadron at RN Air Station Donibristle, at the north end of the Forth Bridge. At first the unit was marking time awaiting pilots and its new Lend-Lease Grumman Martlet (Wildcat) aircraft. During this lull an urgent signal was received from No. 801 Squadron, based at RNAS Hatston

The rugged Skua banking steeply, giving a good view of the flat sturdy wing with the modified, upturned tips.

Below: RNAS Hatston, designated HMS Sparrowhawk, was purpose-built during 1940 as a base for Fleet Air Arm operations. It was unusual in that it was built with four hard runways from the outset rather than the normal three. The site was chosen to be far enough away from enemy airfields to avoid attack.

Below: The aerial view which greeted a very relieved Eric Brown on his return from Bergen; RNAS Hatston, 1941.

Above: Pilots climbing into the cockpits of their Skuas at RNAS Hatston. (© Imperial War Museums A 8218)

Right: Skuas at Hatston, being loaded with anti-personnel bombs in preparation for a mission, with the Bay of Weyland in the background. (© Imperial War Museums A 8222)

in the Orkneys, requesting three Skuas to be ferried there from the Repair Yard Pool. Fletch and I immediately volunteered for the task just to relieve the boredom.

We arrived at Hatston on 11 April 1941, and were more than a little surprised to discover that we were to replace, albeit very temporarily, two 801 Squadron pilots who were not available. The next day we attended a

Mastering the techniques of dive-bombing with Zap flaps deployed. This aircraft, L2883, was one of the Blackburn Skuas flown by 771 Squadron from RNAS Hatston between 1940 and 1943.

briefing for an attack on some oil storage tanks at Bergen in Norway, which was to take place, weather permitting, next morning. Fletch and I were not at all dismayed by this unexpected turn of events. With all the enthusiasm of youth, we were more excited at the prospect of some real action.

The next day had favourable weather, so we were off early. It was a long haul to Norway, running on weak mixture, in a gaggle of twelve. We two new boys carried a squadron observer and a 500 lb bomb. The journey lasted just over two hours, made slightly less tedious by having a companion in the rear seat. The transit was made at 1,500 ft until we sighted the Norwegian coast, and then began the climb to 7,000 ft, which we reached without opposition. We all lined up in the order briefed and I found it absolutely exhilarating to hurtle down on the target, release my bomb and then push down, heading for the exit fjord.

So far so good, but then the whole scenario changed, as a swarm of Bf 109E fighters pounced on us. I made a lightning decision to get right

down on the water and hug the fjord's wall of rock on my starboard side, hopefully restricting our opponent to a difficult astern attack and giving my observer an easy target for his single Lewis gun. However, I was very concerned for his safety, and when he called that the 109 was within firing range I opened the dive flaps, which caused such a rapid deceleration that the German pilot had to take some very sharp evasive action to avoid a collision. The 109 returned for another last go at us from the forward port quarter. He hit us with a short burst of fire, giving me a flesh wound in the left arm and silencing my observer. This really worried me because I didn't know if he was incapacitated or if our voice communication tube had been damaged. In between attacks he had managed to give me a course to steer for the Orkneys, so as we reached the mouth of the fjord I set off in the given direction, greatly relieved that the 109 had apparently given up on us. I then made a quick assessment of our combat damage, being mainly concerned as to whether our long transparent canopy over the cockpits had been

The Blackburn Skua was not the most aerodynamic of aircraft, and I was very concerned that any damage to its greenhouse canopy would seriously increase our fuel consumption. Even running on a lean mixture at slow speed we would have had little chance of making it back to Hatston.

'… he called that the 109 was within firing range, I opened the dive flaps, which caused such a rapid deceleration that the German pilot had to take sharp evasive action to avoid a collision.'

'The 109 returned for another last go at us from the forward port quarter and hit his target…'

smashed, as this would cause severe drag on the flight back which we could ill afford. Luckily the canopy appeared to be intact and the few bullet holes I could see seemed to be concentrated along the fuselage near the canopy sill.

The flight back across the North Sea seemed to take an eternity, and although my arm wound ached it was not bothering me as much as my concern for my observer, and the fact that I could not see any of the other Skuas.

When at last land came in sight, and I recognised the Orkney Islands, I again heaved a huge sigh of relief. I found Hatston Airfield quite easily and landed as quickly as possible. Help was immediately at hand, and I discovered my observer had been slightly wounded like me. He had lapsed into unconsciousness, but was soon revived on reaching the sick bay. It transpired that he had ducked down low in the cockpit when we were under fire and had received a grazed bullet wound to his temple, which had totally concussed him.

Happily I was reunited with Fletch, who had evaded the enemy fighters, probably because

Above: The Skua operated mainly in the North Sea and had some success during the Norwegian campaign, when aircraft from 800 and 803 Squadrons sank the German cruiser Konigsburg *in Bergen harbour.*

Left: The Blackburn Skua had a short active career. It first flew in 1937 but was retired from front-line service in 1941 after suffering severe losses against the more advanced German fighters.

The head-on view of a Bf 109. Staring down the barrel of its propeller-hub cannon is not something a pilot forgets, and few have survived. Luckily he opened fire with his wing-mounted machine-guns and caused only minimal damage.

he was one of the first wave of attackers and had cleared the target area well before me. The raid was a great success and the German oil storage tanks were totally destroyed, with no loss of aircraft or crew.

We eventually returned to Donibristle, where our Martlets were now arriving, and after a brief work-up we embarked in the escort carrier HMS *Audacity*. On our very first convoy protection run Fletch distinguished himself by sharing in the kill of a heavily armed, four-engined Focke-Wulf Fw 200 Kurier. Sadly he himself was shot down and killed by a surfaced U-boat on 17 December 1941.

Eyeball-to-eyeball with a 'Condor'

Two for the price of one – if you do your homework

8 November 1941

Eyeball-to-eyeball with a 'Condor'

Two for the price of one – if you do your homework

When I joined 802 Squadron of Martlet (Lend-Lease) aircraft in early 1941 our Squadron Commander, John Wintour, started organising his young pilots by giving us specific responsibilities associated with squadron activities. I was delighted to be made Armament Officer, with responsibility for the maintenance, harmonisation and arming of our aircraft guns, as well as the welfare of our groundcrew armourers. The Martlets were fitted with 0.5 in.-calibre Colt-Browning machine-guns, and therefore new to the Fleet Air Arm. Previously, all our aircraft had been equipped with the lighter Vickers or Browning 0.303 in. guns. Not only did the Martlet offer much greater firepower, but also had the advantage that, if the guns jammed, they could be recocked from inside the cockpit. The original Mk I Martlets we

An aerial view of RNAS Donibristle, where we rookies of 802 Squadron did our training on the newly arrived Grumman Martlets, and our first tentative land-based attempts at deck landing. There were no dummy wires across the runway at Donibristle, we were just expected to touch down in line with the batsman, who was our guide on approach. (FAA Museum)

A diagram of the Fw 200 Kurier's defensive arsenal and the relative fields of fire. It highlights the head-on 'window of opportunity' first exploited by Eric Brown and the pilots flying from HMS Audacity.

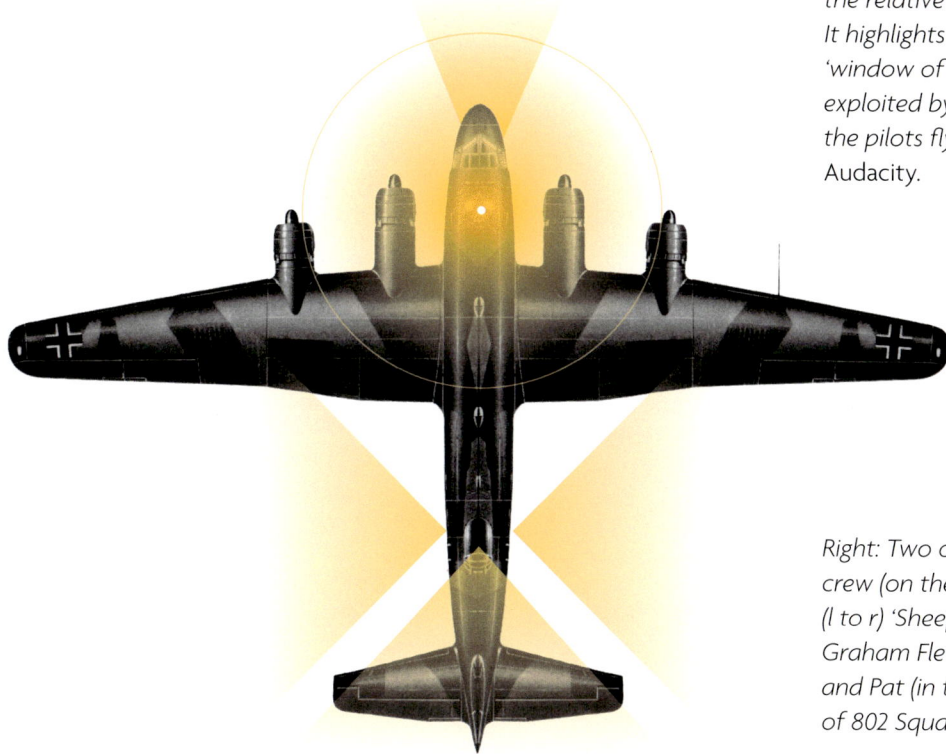

Right: Two of our ground crew (on the wing) and (l to r) 'Sheepy' Lamb, Graham Fletcher, Bertie and Pat (in the cockpit) of 802 Squadron.

received were fitted with four wing-mounted 0.5 in. guns, but in mid-1941 these aircraft were replaced by the six-gun Mk II version.

Once aboard *Audacity*, John Wintour organised the squadron into two flights, which were then subdivided into four sections, He and Hutch Hutchinson made up Blue section, Sheepy Lamb and I were Red, Phil Morris and John Carden were Green and Pat Paterson and Fletch formed Black

As an extra duty I took on the task of examining the vulnerability of our main

WITH 802 FIGHTER SQUADRON AT DONIBRISTLE. SHEEPY, FLETCH, BERTIE AND PAT (IN COCKPIT).

Below: The Focke-Wulf Fw 200 had a formidable reputation amongst the Allied convoys, having been responsible for the loss of 85 vessels and 363,000 tons of shipping in just six months between August 1940 and February 1941.

predicted foe in the Battle of the Atlantic – the Focke-Wulf Fw 200 Kurier, the military version of the civil Condor airliner. The Kurier was very heavily armed to compensate for its peaceful origins. Its defensive armour consisted of an underbelly gondola with a 20 mm cannon in the nose firing forwards and downwards through a 55-degree angle of depression and with a lateral traverse of 28 degrees each side of its central axis, and another cannon firing aft and downwards with similar angles of movement. A third cannon in a powered turret immediately aft of the flight deck was capable of rotating through a full 360 degrees. However, with a lack of any firm data I had to make a calculated guess at its possible angle of depression without shooting off the aircraft's own nose or tail. Finally there was a 13 mm gun on a Scarff-ring-type mounting firing from an aft dorsal

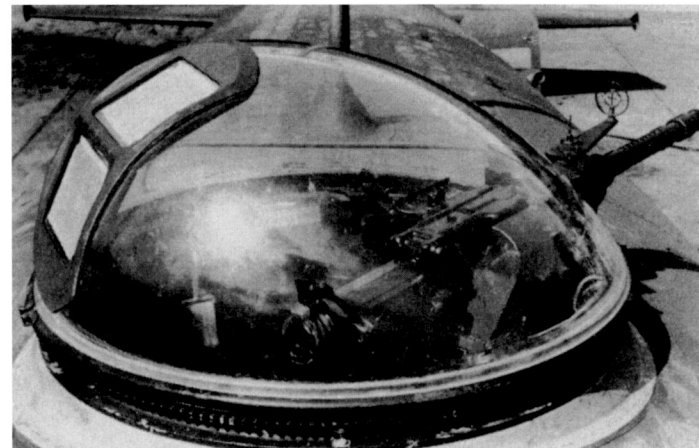

Left: The hydraulically-operated Fw 19 forward upper turret (A-stand), mounting a single 7.9 mm MG 15 machine-gun, was introduced on the Fw 200C-3 and replaced the fixed raised fairing featured on earlier sub-types.

This view of HMS Searcher, *one of the smaller Ruler-class escort carriers, pitching in stormy seas, gives a harrowing reminder of the challenges faced by the pilots who flew from them.*

A photograph taken at RNAS Donibristle in 1939. Sheepy Lamb, my Red-section leader on Audacity, *is standing in the centre, to his right is Mike Fell who went on to become an Admiral, and seated on the right is Alec Fraser-Harris, an expert on dive-bombing who was our instructor in the art, flying Skuas at Donibristle. (FAA Museum)*

Below: A Martlet takes off from HMS Searcher, *one of the Royal Navy's escort carriers. The flight deck of these carriers varied in size, but* Audacity's *was less than twice the wingspan of a Grumman Martlet – not an easy target to land on in mid-Atlantic.*

position. This powerful armament could be supplemented by 7.9 mm hand-held machine guns firing through side windows. Sizing all this up, I concluded that the best chance of success against a Kurier was an absolutely flat head-on approach aiming at the cockpit from a firing range of 600 yds closing to some 200 yds, finishing with a violent steep breakaway upwards in either direction. I discussed this with my fellow pilots, but they felt this limited us to a one-shot attack. Once the breakaway was made, both the attacker and target were departing in opposite directions and were unlikely to renew contact. To sum up, they were interested but not overly enthusiastic. However, this attitude was shortly to change, with dramatic results.

Below: A rare shot of HMS Audacity *at sea with six Martlets lashed down on the aft flight deck. Because* Audacity *had no hangar, the ground crew bravely carried out all the repairs and maintenance on the open deck, often in appalling conditions.(FAA Museum)*

The first opportunity to test my head-on theory came during convoy OG 76, which left the Clyde on 29 October 1941, bound for Gibraltar. 802 Squadron joined it aboard the new escort carrier HMS *Audacity*, with our eight Martlets firmly lashed to the flight deck. We were attacked by Kuriers and U-boats as soon as we entered the Bay of Biscay, and on the morning of 8 November our squadron CO, John Wintour, was shot down by the Kurier he was attacking. About an hour and a half later that afternoon, having had little time to reflect on this disaster, my Section Leader 'Sheepy' Lamb and I were off on a Kurier chase. We had run through our stock of Martlets to such an extent that the captain had asked me if I would fly one with a slightly bent propeller blade caused by an over enthusiastic group of mechanics pushing two of our machines into each other when clearing the flight deck to receive the surviving Martlet from John Wintour's section. There was no hesitation on my part, as we were all in an angry mood.

Sheepy eventually spotted two Kuriers flying under a layer of scudding cloud and decided we should attack them separately. As soon as

An almost impossible approach, but one of the few safe angles of attack on a Kurier if you managed to stay below the fire of the forward gondola gun. (RAF Museum Hendon P012145)

The Focke-Wulf Fw 200 Kurier was a formidable foe, scouring the Atlantic for Allied convoys and passing their locations to the German U-boat packs. They played a key role in the loss of over 14 million tons of shipping during the war.

the Germans became aware of us, a cat-and-mouse chase in and out of the cloud ensued. The cloud was not thick, so I stayed on top, believing this would give me the best chance of keeping in contact with my prey. After much frustration, and thinking I had lost him, he suddenly broke cover about 500 yds almost dead ahead of me, so I kept flat and blazed away as I headed towards what seemed an inevitable collision with this massive target.

I knew that if I missed this time I would never see him again, so I hung on until the very last second. It was close enough to see the big windscreen round the two German pilots shatter. The huge machine reared, stalled and spiralled into the sea. Sheepy was not so lucky, and lost his Kurier in cloud.

On the returning convoy HG76 on the morning of 19 December we were under heavy attack from U-boats and Kuriers, and Sheepy

Michael Turner '14

Left: The 20mm cannon in the underbelly gondola had a limited field of fire, and proved ineffective against our head-on attacks.

Below: The Kurier was heavily defended and had exceptional range.

and I found ourselves directed against two more of the four-engined giants. We attacked them separately and both used our new-found head-on technique. I had instant success and watched my second Kurier crash into the water. Unfortunately Sheepy did not get a direct run-in, but still managed to inflict severe damage on his opponent, which escaped in the cloud.

In the same afternoon we had another Kurier visit and it was intercepted by two of our remaining Martlets. They made a number of unsuccessful stern attacks before the section leader made a last desperate head-on attack and pushed it so close he struck the Kurier's wing on his breakaway and came back to *Audacity* with part of the Kurier's port aileron attached to his tailwheel. That was *Audacity's* swansong, for on 21 December 1941 she was sunk by U-751 with heavy loss of life, but with a countering score of five Kuriers and assists in the destruction of five U-boats.

The sinking of
HMS *Audacity*

Adrift in the freezing
North Atlantic

21 December 1941

The sinking of HMS *Audacity*

Adrift in the freezing Atlantic

In February 1940 the German cargo boat SS *Hannover* was captured in the Caribbean, where it had been operating as a banana carrier. It was intercepted off St Domingo by the cruiser HMS *Dunedin* and the Canadian destroyer HMCS *Assiniboine* and towed to Jamaica. It eventually arrived in Britain, where at the Blyth shipyard north of Newcastle in Northumberland it was to present Prime Minister Churchill with the opportunity to realise one of his brainwaves.

His idea was to slice the superstructure off the 5,537-ton vessel and superimpose an unobstructed flight deck, creating a small aircraft carrier which could escort convoys during the Battle of the Atlantic. Although having no hangar to house them, it would carry up to eight fighter aircraft lashed down at the tail end of the flight deck, which was only 420 ft long and 60 ft wide.

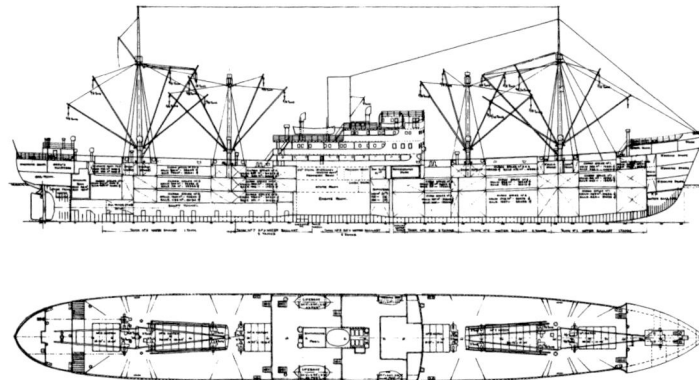

Above & left: The SS Hannover *was captured by the Royal Navy in 1940 off the coast of the Dominican Republic. The following year it was converted to become one of the first escort carriers and renamed* Empire Audacity *and finally* HMS Audacity. *Evaluation plans were prepared prior to conversion. (Drawing: FAA Museum)*

Above: HMS Audacity *embarks in its final convoy HG76 en route from Gibraltar.* (© Imperial War Museums HU 54361)

Right: HMS Puncher *followed much the same design as* Audacity *apart from the addition of a small island on the starboard side.*

It operated successfully in protecting four convoys from Liverpool to Gibraltar between September and the 21 December 1941, when it was sunk in the Bay of Biscay.

On that fateful day I was the last pilot to land my Martlet aboard *Audacity*, at 19:20 in the gathering dusk. At 20:33 I was happily eating my evening meal in the tiny wardroom when a major U-boat attack was launched against the convoy. In defence *Audacity* was zigzagging at its full 14 knots, clear of the convoy's five columns of ships, when a torpedo blew off the rudder and the ship had to heave-to and stop to avoid colliding with other ships in the darkness.

Some 25 minutes after the first torpedo hit, U-751 surfaced about 200 yds from *Audacity's* port beam. The submarine was covered in phosphorescence, which glowed eerily in the dark. The U-boat commander could be seen on the conning tower, sizing-up the situation, and meanwhile our captain had ordered all crew to muster on the flight deck with lifebelts. After about five minutes one of the sailors, on his own initiative, suddenly leapt for an Oerlikon gun mounted on the port side and started firing at the U-boat.

The German reaction was virtually instantaneous, and we could plainly see the white bubbling tracks of two more torpedoes coming at us. Everyone rushed toward the starboard side of the flight deck, then both torpedoes hit the bows of *Audacity*. There was a tremendous explosion, probably of aviation fuel, and the whole of the forward quarter of the ship disappeared. Split seconds later the rest of the ship reared up so steeply we could barely keep our feet. I was near the aircraft lashed down aft, and above the other noises heard the frightening sound of the wire lashings whining under the impossible strain. They all seemed to part simultaneously with a great twang, and the aircraft plunged down the

Above: The author prepares for take-off from Audacity.

Right: Hot-shot fighter pilots. Top is Bertie, then me inverted and below is Fletch; on a flight from Audacity *to Gibraltar.*

'I struck out to get away from the suction effect of the sinking ship, and when I last saw Audacity it was plunging almost vertically to its grave.'

A newspaper cutting from Eric Brown's scrapbook records the events surrounding convoy HG76's return journey from Gibraltar in December 1941.

NAVY LOSES FOUR SHIPS

Convoy Escort Hits Back

Three U-Boats Sunk; Bombers Destroyed

TWO ADMIRALTY COMMUNIQUES ISSUED TO-DAY ANNOUNCE THE LOSS OF A BRITISH CRUISER, TWO DESTROYERS, AND AN AUXILIARY VESSEL.

THE CRUISER (H.M.S. NEPTUNE) AND THE DESTROYER KANDAHAR WERE VICTIMS OF ENEMY MINES IN THE MEDITERRANEAN.

THE OTHER TWO VESSELS WERE LOST DURING AN ATTACK BY U-BOATS ON AN ATLANTIC CONVOY WHICH LASTED FIVE DAYS.

THE HUNS PAID DEARLY FOR THIS ATTACK, HOW-EVER, AS THREE U-BOATS AT LEAST WERE SUNK, WHILE TWO NAZI LONG-RANGE BOMBERS WERE SENT HEADLONG INTO THE SEA AND A THIRD WAS SEVERELY DAMAGED. ONLY TWO MERCHANT SHIPS FROM A CONVOY OF 30 WERE SUNK.

Here is the full story of the attack on the convoy, as told in an Admiralty communique issued this afternoon:

"Week after week our convoys continue to arrive, bringing vital supplies to our shores. Among those which arrived recently was one which was subjected to an exceptionally determined and sustained attack both by U-boats and long-range aircraft.

"Over 90 per cent. of the merchant shipping tonnage in that convoy arrived safely, and serious losses were inflicted upon the enemy by the convoy escorts.

"It is known that at least three of the attacking U-boats were sunk, since prisoners of war from three U-boats were taken.

"Two of the German long-range Focke-Wulfe aircraft were shot down into the sea, and a third was severely damaged and may not have regained its base.

LEADERS HONOURED

"The successful passage of the convoy and the losses inflicted upon the enemy were not, how-ever, achieved without loss to the convoy escorts, and the Board of

Admiralty regrets to announce that the ex-American destroyer Stanley (Lieut.-Commander D. B. Shaw, O.B.E., R.N.) and the auxiliary vessel H.M.S. Audacity (CVmmander D. W. Mackendrick, R.N.) were sunk.

"The next-of-kin of casualties in these ships' companies have been informed.

"The convoy consisted of more than 30 merchant ships, with Vice-Admiral Raymond Fitzmaurice, D.S.O., as Commodore. Vice-Admiral Fitzmaurice has seen much service as commodore of convoys during the present war, and he was appointed K.B.E. in the New Year honours for this work.

"The senior officer of the convoy escorts was Commander F. J. Walker, R.N., in H.M.S. Stork. Commander Walker has been awarded the D.S.O. for his service with this convoy.

DEPTH CHARGES DID IT

"The attack on the convoy developed on December 17, and before noon on that day the first U-boat was sunk. The U-boat was sighted on the surface, and was sunk by gunfire from ships of the escort. The prisoners taken from this U-boat stated that it had been forced to the surface by damage inflicted in depth charge attacks earlier in the day.

"That afternoon two Focke-Wulfe aircraft approached the convoy. They were engaged and driven off by naval aircraft from H.M.S. Audacity.

"Next day the attack by U-boats was continued, the escorts counter-attacked strongly and successfully and another U-boat was forced to the surface by depth charges and then sank. Some of the crew of this U-boat have survived as prisoners of war.

"Some hours later the ex-American destroyer H.M.S. Stanley, which had taken part in the destruction of this second U-boat, was herself torpedoed and sunk. The other escorts countered with heavy depth-charge attacks, and yet another U-boat was forced to the surface. It was rammed and sunk by H.M.S. Stork, some prisoners being taken.

BOMBERS' FATE

"On December 19 three Focke Wulfe aircraft approached the convoy and endeavoured to attack it. They were at once engaged by naval aircraft from H.M.S. Audacity. Two of the Focke Wulfe were shot down into the sea, and the third was badly damaged and driven off.

"For the next few days the enemy continued to attack the convoy with U-boats. During this time H.M.S. Audacity, one of the auxiliary vessels provided for the defence of convoys against German long-range aircraft, was torpedoed and sunk.

"Throughout these two days the remaining U-boats were relentlessly hunted and heavily depth-charged by convoy escorts. On December 21 the attack was finally broken off.

"American-built Liberator air-craft of Coastal Command of the R.A.F. joined the convoy at this stage and played a conspicuous part in the final series of counter-attacks, which eventually freed the convoy from further pursuit."

The U-boat U-751 docked in St Nazaire, one of the German Navy's main submarine bases on the Atlantic coast of France.

Kapitan Gerhard Bigalk commanded U-751 from June 1941 until 17 July 1942, when it was sunk with all hands by depth charges dropped by a Whitley from 502 Squadron RAF and a Lancaster from 61 Squadron RAF in the North Atlantic, north-west of Cape Ortegal, Spain.

wildly tilting deck as if in formation. There was a jarring, broken crash as they hit each other and then splayed out over the deck. The cries and screams of men being mowed down by the monsters mingled with the warning shouts, including my own, as I leapt into the starboard catwalk. Many leapt straight off the flight deck into the sea, a long jump from the now steeply-angled deck, and were badly hurt on impact.

By now clad in my leather Irvine flying jacket and flying boots over my uniform, topped off with my Mae West, I made my way to the promenade deck, where I nipped into my cabin to pick up my precious flying log book before jumping overboard some twenty feet into the sea. It was now dotted everywhere with struggling bodies. I immediately felt weighed down by my flying boots and kicked them off and let my log book go as it was restricting my movement, being tucked under my jacket. So lightened, I struck out to get away from the suction effect of the sinking ship, and when I last saw *Audacity* it was plunging almost vertically to its grave.

I now had to depend for survival on my trusty Mae West, as a few of our escorting corvettes came to pick up survivors but turned away before getting to the small group I was with. This was a prudent move, as I learned later, they had been warned that U-boats were still in the area. The end result was a wait of some three hours for rescue and the loss of most of the group, who were equipped only with lifebelts and not with Mae Wests.

HMS *Audacity*'s short career was not in vain, as its aircraft shot down five heavily armed Focke-Wulf Fw 200 Kurier reconnaissance bombers and assisted in the detection and destruction of five U-boats. The success of these so-called 'Woolworth' carriers caused a major headache for Germany's U-boat command, who realised that escort carriers would be used against them from thenceforth.

One of the most reassuring sights Eric Brown ever saw, HMS Convolvulus *eventually picked him up after three freezing hours in the Atlantic.* (© Imperial War Museums FL 6066)

Corkscrewing a Halifax

Solving a problem for
Bomber Command
under the scrutiny of a
Master Bomber

14 April 1944

Corkscrewing a Halifax

Solving a problem for Bomber Command under the scrutiny of a Master Bomber

In 1943 the four-engined Handley Page Halifax bomber was a major component of Bomber Command's night operations against Germany. Although, it was normally an exceptionally reliable aircraft, it suffered an unusual number of losses apparently due to loss of control during corkscrew manoeuvres. The corkscrew was a fairly violent manoeuvre used to evade searchlights or nightfighters, and consisted of a turning dive to about 300 mph then an upward spiral in the opposite direction, followed by a wing-over into a downward spiral with a strong pull-out and turn back into level flight. Before this last action, speed had built up in the dive, so the rudder forces were particularly heavy in the recovery turn. As the pilot reached two-thirds travel on the stick the forces would suddenly lighten and lock over to full travel, causing a dramatic loss of control.

The Halifax Mk II, the Lancaster and Wellington formed the backbone of Bomber Command for much of the war.

In early 1944 I had been involved in some exploratory flight tests to investigate this problem. It was also being examined by Handley Page and Bomber Command, and finally resulted in the replacement of the triangular fins with larger rectangular units. The Royal Aircraft Establishment (RAE) at Farnborough was required to carry out the final tests and issue the approval for this modification. To make these flights more realistic they took place over nearby Laffan's Plain, where the Army would man searchlights, and Bomber Command was to send a senior operational pilot to act as observer. I was given the demonstration task, presumably because of

my participation in the earlier trials, and on the chosen day, awaited the 'bomber boy' who was to fly with us on the test. I was completely taken aback when it turned out to be none other than the famed Wing Commander Leonard Cheshire, VC.

Pilot Officer Leonard Cheshire with his flight and ground crew in front of their aircraft named Offenbach, and, left, as a Group Captain in 1945 with ribbons for the VC and DFC. (RAF Museum Hendon P000688)

MZ523

Michael Turner '14

APR. 1550	13	AIRACOBRA	A H 574	SELF	—	AIR TEST. Hooked naval version.
APR. 1700	13	HURRICANE IV	K Z 706	SELF	—	WEATHER TEST. 2-260 lbs. rocket projectiles fitted.
APR. 1740	13	SPITFIRE XIII	B L 348	SELF	—	SPEED COURSE TESTS.
APR. 0930	14	HURRICANE IV	K Z 706	SELF	—	LEVELS
APR. 1140	14	'M.18 II	J N 403	SELF	P./O. SAIGER	HIGH LIFT COEFFICIENT.
APR. 1445	14	HALIFAX III	M Z 523	SELF	2 CREW	HANDLING. Corkscrews with modified tail. W/C Cheshire aboard.
APR. 1140	15	SEAFIRE L IIc	M B 307	SELF	—	2 R.A.T.O.s
APR. 1600	15	ANSON	R 9864	F./O. BUCK	SELF	FARNBOROUGH TO MACHRIHANISH.
APR. 1005	17	SEAFIRE XV	N S 487	SELF	—	MACHRIHANISH TO WEST FREUGH. Low cloud. Vis 3000 yds.

Left: The entry in Eric Brown's logbook for the corkscrew demonstration in Halifax Mk III MZ523.

Below left: Halifax Mk III HX227, with the modified rectangular fins.

Below: A diagram of the corkscrew manoeuvre. The aircraft's problems usually occurred at the bottom of the dive as the pilot pulled out and banked into the climb.

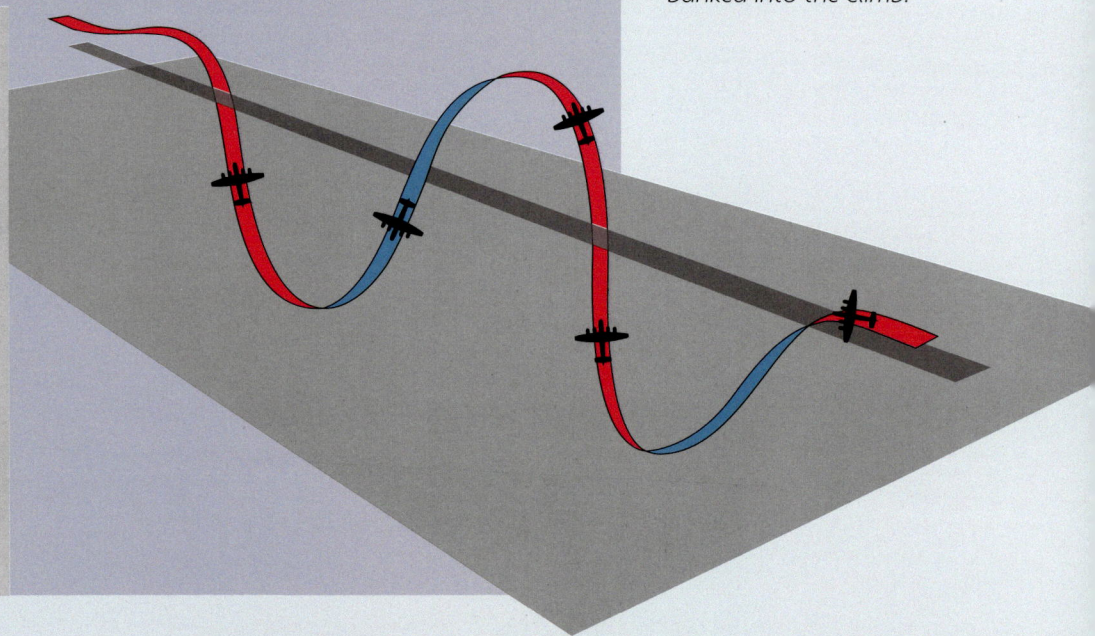

A Bomber Command Lancaster on a night raid over Germany nears its target, silhouetted by searchlights, flares and flak. Their final approach had to be made straight and level, making them particularly vulnerable to anti-aircraft fire from the ground.

His presence did not overawe me, but it certainly made me aware I was under expert scrutiny. However, he very unobtrusively positioned himself just behind my right shoulder and clipped himself into a specially prepared RAE retaining harness. I was also conscious that our scenario was missing certain elements the bomber boys took for granted, namely flak and fighters, but I was determined that this would not detract from the objective of the flight.

We carried out the first corkscrew to the left, and Cheshire seemed quite satisfied with the recovery action but made no comments.

I then said to him that, if he really wanted to see how effective the new tail was, he should close an outer throttle lever without warning at some stage near the highest point of the next corkscrew. I then initiated a corkscrew to the right and, just as I started the wing-over, he pulled the throttle of the port outer engine back to fully closed. As we lost the thrust effect I had to apply heavy force to the right rudder, but we rotated smoothly over the top, but I then had to apply even heavier rudder at the escape stage. During the whole manoeuvre Cheshire stood quite impassive, and I could not gauge any reaction from his face as we were both wearing tinted-lens goggles to preserve our night vision against the searchlight beams.

After the demonstration flight we landed back at Farnborough and I asked the great man if he had any concerns about the flight. With a deadpan expression he replied: 'Yes, being flown in a Bomber Command heavy by a pilot in naval uniform'. He then shook me warmly by the hand before departing for a debrief with RAE boffins.

Although the modification to the Halifax fins greatly increased the safety of the corkscrew manoeuvre, there remained a considerable risk of disaster if the aircraft was mishandled in the event of an engine failure at a critical stage of the manoeuvre, when a fatal spin could be the end result.

An early Mk II Halifax with square wingtips, Merlin engines and an H2S radar housing below the fuselage. It has also been retrofitted with the modified rectangular fins.

Murphy's Law . . .

. . . .if there is anything
that can go wrong, then
be sure it will

10 July 1944

Murphy's Law...

…If there is anything that can go wrong, then be sure it will

In the early days of the Battle of the Atlantic desperate measures were sought to reduce the dreadful attrition rate to Allied shipping caused by German U-boat attacks. These losses mainly occurred in the middle 1,000-mile zone of the 3,000-mile gap between Great Britain and the USA, just beyond the range of Allied maritime aircraft. However, the Germans operated the military version of the Focke-Wulf Fw 200 Condor civil airliner which had the necessary radius of action to reach that crucial area. They performed a dual role, searching out the convoys and bombing them, and then reporting their position to the U-boat wolf-packs which then closed in for a bonanza of destruction.

British Prime Minister Winston Churchill applied his mind to this problem and came up with the concept of the Catapult Armed

The realisation of Churchill's dream, a Hurricane mounted on the catapult launch track of a CAM ship.

Right: The CAM ship SS Empire Tide *at anchor, awaiting convoy duty with a Hurricane mounted on the catapult launch gantry fitted to the bow. FO P J Flynn shot down a Focke-Wulf Fw 200 Kurier after being launched from* Empire Tide *on 28 July 1943.*

Below: A dramatic dusk shot of a rocket powered catapult take-off by a Hurricane.

Merchant Ship (CAM Ship), a merchant ship fitted with a rocket catapult which could launch a fighter aircraft.

The strategy was to place a CAM Ship within a convoy and, in the event of an alert, it would wait until the enemy aircraft was actually spotted before launching a Fulmar or Hurricane fighter. The main drawback to this plan was that, once catapulted, the pilot could not return to the ship, but would have to make land if it was within range or move in close to the convoy and ditch in the sea or bale out in the hope of being picked up by one of the escort vessels.

From 1942 I became involved with testing the fighter catapults at sea and, later in 1944, on shore at RAE Farnborough, where the development and design of new catapults took place.

With the passage of time it was becoming clear that the improved performance of German maritime aircraft would necessitate upgrading our catapult fighters, and the obvious choice was to replace the Hurricane with the Spitfire.

We had already carried out successful trials in early 1944 when a message was received that Winston Churchill himself would like to witness a Spitfire rocket catapult launch demonstration. When the appointed day dawned there was quite a buzz of excitement around the RAE at the prospect of impressing the great man.

The rocket catapult was mounted on an elevated track and consisted of a trolley with four legs to receive catapult spools fitted on the aircraft's fuselage. At the front of the trolley at track level were two long steel spikes, and at the rear a battery of 18 rocket motors. At the end of the track were two retardation barrels filled with water contained by a frangible disc, which when penetrated by the spikes brought the trolley to a halt in 10 ft and allowed the trolley legs to collapse forward and release the aircraft.

The man responsible for filling the retardation barrels was a genial Irishman aptly named Mr Murphy, but on this auspicious day he was rather overawed by the occasion and forgot to fill the barrels. When the launch was

Hawker Sea Hurricane Mark I Z4936 'KE-M', of the Merchant Ship Fighter Unit is lowered on to the catapult at Speke, Liverpool, for a training launch. At the back of the catapult are some of the rockets used to power the launch cradle. (© Imperial War Museums CH 15390)

Hurricane Z4936 is fired from the catapult with its cockpit canopy open, which was standard practice for all naval pilots in case they ditched on take-off and needed to leave the aircraft quickly.

Michael Turner

Date		Aircraft Type	No.	Pilot	Crew	Remarks
Jul. 1500	4	Barracuda II	LS540	Self	Mr Stott	Take-Off Acceleration Measurements.
Jul. 1545	4	Walrus	L2219	Self	2 Crew	Tail Wheel Shimmy. T.C. type fitted. Landed at Reading.
Jul. 1030	10	Wildcat V	JV330	Self	—	2 A.T.Os. Proof testing S.C.1s for accelerating. 2 S.C.1s fitted.
Jul. 1210	10	Wellington XIII	MF232	Self	2 Crew	Cabin Heating Duct Temperature Measurements.
Jul. 1530	10	Seafire IIC	MB299	Self	—	Rocket High Catapult. Demonstration to buzz bomb investigators. ✱✱✱ Very spectacular! Some clot forgot to fill trolley buffers with water with result that the Seafire + ½ ton trolley became airborne together. Fortunately trolley broke clear to prang on runway.
Jul. 1030	11	Lancaster III	ED842	Self	5 Crew	Undercarriage Reactions. Strain gauge readings for 3 bumps.
Jul. 1155	11	Wildcat V	JV330	Self	—	A.T.O. with S.C.1s fitted.
Jul. 1540	11	Firebrand	DK366	Self	—	Farnborough to Hullavington and Return.
Jul. 0940	12	Typhoon IB	EK154	Self	—	Levels.

'Some clot forgot to fill the trolley buffers with water…'

Above: A busy day at the office – Eric Brown's log book records; RATOG (Rocket Assisted Take-off Gear) trials on a Wildcat Mk V, cabin heating measurements on a Wellington and the ill-fated catapult launch tests in a Seafire IIC.

Right: The Seafire IIC MA970.

Above & right: Just eleven days before Eric Brown's mishap, Seafire IIc MA970, on the P.I catapult trolley at RAE Farnborough, 30 June 1942. (Farnborough Air Sciences)

Right: The rocket assembly which powered the trolley, armed and ready. (Farnborough Air Sciences)

made, it initially seemed normal until there was a sharp jolt at peak 'g'. At first I thought something had ripped the undercarriage off the Seafire IIC I was flying, but I had instinctively gone through the retraction procedure and found no difficulty. Then, for a fleeting moment, I sensed that the Seafire was not accelerating as it should and was sinking instead of climbing, so I kept the throttle wide open until I suddenly felt the aircraft jump up in the same way a bomber does when it drops its bomb load.

All this was witnessed by the Prime Minister, who apparently did not comment on the incident, much to the relief of the catapult crew. However, there was no rush to substitute the Seafire for the Hurricat, as the catapult Hurricane was affectionately known, because the ditching characteristics of the Seafire resembled those of a submarine.

Later in 1944 I was conducting similar tests when I noticed a slight RAF officer in the uniform of a Group Captain watching with great interest. After completion of the tests he approached me, introduced himself as Frank Whittle, and said he was interested in catapulting as he had been very involved in such work at the Marine Aircraft Experimental Establishment at Felixstowe as a test pilot in 1931. I reminded him that I had witnessed the first flight of his Gloster E.28/39 at Cranwell in 1941 and said that I had just been appointed to the Jet Flight at RAE. It was the beginning of a lifelong friendship with this man of genius.

Left: The right way to leave the catapult.

Below: The wrong way to do it. Eric Brown's ill-fated attempt as witnessed by Winston Churchill.

Unscheduled exit

The fiery bale-out that ended as a load of bull

26 July 1944

Unscheduled exit

The fiery bale-out that ended as a load of bull

In the summer of 1944 England was subjected to an onslaught of German V1 pilotless flying bombs launched from inclined ramp sites, mainly in occupied France and Belgium. These V1s were powered by an impulse-duct jet engine giving a thrust of some 600 lb and producing a virtually constant speed of 400 mph over a distance of 150 miles. The operational height was normally 1,000 to 2,500 ft, although some were reported as reaching 7,000 ft. The bomb load was an explosive charge of 1,870 lb. The V1 was controlled in flight by an autopilot, and its range could be pre-set to put the device into its final destructive dive over a predetermined target.

In June 1944 my wife and I had our home in Aldershot hit by a V1 early in the morning. The bomb actually landed on our dog's kennel in

Left: The underground V1 assembly lines were situated in Northern France.

Below left: The ominous silence following the constant drone of an incoming V1 caused alarm all over London as it plunged on to its target.

Opposite: The Mustang III (top), the Spitfire XIV (below), which along with the Tempest V, were the only Allied aircraft capable of chasing the V1s as they crossed the Channel.

the back garden, but the two-storey house collapsed like a pack of cards. The bomb slightly injured my wife, seriously hurt our cleaning lady, who lost an eye, and killed our golden retriever. From here on I had a score to settle with the V1.

The RAF was finding the 'buzz bomb' a difficult threat to counter, as none of our current fighters could match its speed at low level. In response RAE Farnborough initiated a crash programme to improve the low-level performance of the Spitfire XIV, Tempest V and Mustang III. This centred on the development of a 150-octane aromatic fuel, which produced abnormally high power ratios for strictly limited short bursts.

During these trials I was flying Tempest V JN735, powered by a 2,400 hp Napier Sabre IIB on the evening of 26 July, and had completed a 5 min level run at +9 lb boost and 3,450 rpm, which was the maximum obtainable. I then climbed through cloud to 6,000 ft, where the second run was made under similar conditions.

The third run was made at 7,000 ft, at which height only +8 lb boost was obtainable at full throttle, and after 3½ min I detected a slight smell of burning from the floor of the cockpit. A quick check of the engine instruments showed anything but good news, so I throttled back and asked for an emergency homing, which I was given. I flew on this course, maintaining height and low engine settings until I thought I was near base, then began my descent through the solid cloud below (the top was at 5,800 ft and the base at 2,300 ft).

On entering the darkness of the cloud I could see the whole top engine cowling glowing hot, although this had not been visible from the cockpit in the bright sunshine above the cloud. However, the engine was still running, so I continued the descent, but before I broke cloud the engine began to misfire badly and the propeller started to overspeed. I immediately pulled the constant-speed lever back to the fully-coarse stop, but the revs reached 4,200 rpm and then there was a loud bang followed by a spray of oil which covered the windscreen.

In order to see out I had to unbuckle my safety harness and peer round the opaque

Above: Tempest V EJ743 on a pre-delivery flight test before joining 3 Squadron RAF.

Left: On the front line in the battle against the 'doodlebug', Flt Sgt Morris Rose of 3 Squadron briefs fellow pilots on the best methods of attack. He downed his first V1 on 16 June, and by the end of July had claimed a total of 11 destroyed. (© Imperial War Museums CH 13428)

'The flames were creeping into the Tempest's cockpit through the floor around the rudder pedals.'

The distinctive chin radiator of the Sabre II engined Tempest V. Its excellent low-altitude performance made it particularly effective against the German V1s. Out of a total of 9,782 launched against London, the RAF's Tempest squadrons managed to destroy 638. Note the Seafire on the rocket-launch rail in the background.

windscreen. The propeller had seized solid, and the fire under the cowling had now burst out into intense white flames which were also creeping into the cockpit through the floor near the rudder pedals. The heat around my feet hastened my decision to abandon the aircraft.

I removed my helmet and trimmed the Tempest for level flight at 1,600 ft and 170 mph, then stood up on the seat and put my left leg over the port side of the cockpit. I reached inside to pull the stick hard over towards me, so that when the aircraft reached an angle of bank of about 60 degrees I could kick myself free. The altimeter had reached 1,200 ft when I glanced at it as I grabbed the control column spade grip.

When I pulled the parachute ripcord I could see I was heading for open fields, but I was hardly ready for the touchdown, because I was focusing on the Tempest circling around me before it hit the ground and exploded some 200 yds from a small pond, into which I 'splashed' down. From this point the drama gave way to pure comedy.

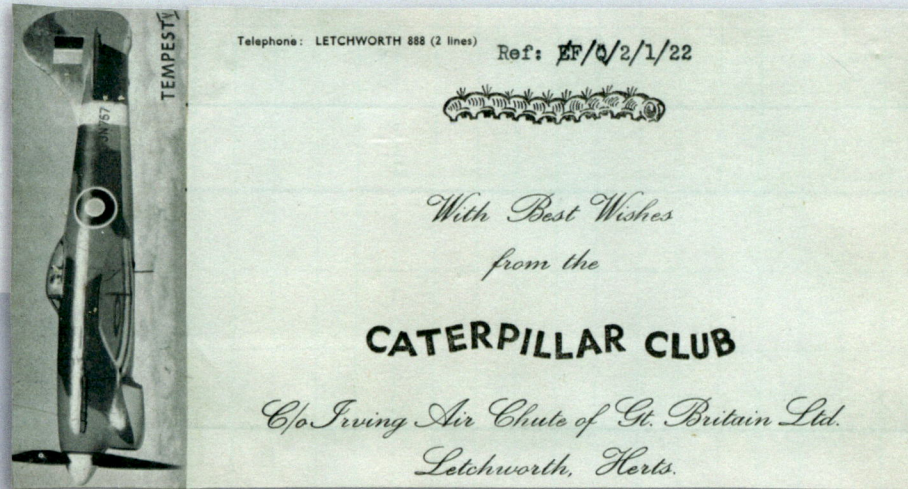

Membership of the Caterpillar Club was awarded by Irving Air Chute of Great Britain Ltd to all pilots who used their parachutes after baling out.

Jul. 1435	25	Fortress	A N 531	Self	4 Crew	Turret Heater Test. Bags of thunder clouds.
Jul. 1650	25	Seafire IIc	M B 125	Self	—	Effect of Throttle Cutting on Powered Descent.
Jul. 0950	26	Lancaster III	N D 743	Self	4 Crew	Trim Curves.
Jul. 1455	26	Seafire IIc	M B 125	Self	—	Effect of Throttle Cutting on Powered Descent.
Jul. 1435	26	Spitfire VA	X 4258	Self	—	Fighter Defence Scramble.
Jul. 1515	26	Firebrand	D K 366	Self	—	Farnborough to West Malling and Return.
Jul. 1845	26	Tempest V	J N 735	Self	—	Levels at +9 lbs. boost. Engine blew up and caught fire; prop. overspeed and seized, so stepped out at 1,000' at 170 mph.
Jul. 1105	27	Seafire IIc	M B 125	Self	—	Effect of Throttle Opening on Powered Descent.
Jul. 1440	27	Beaufighter II	T 3032	Self	Mr. Day	Vertical Velocity Research.
Jul. 1635	27	Libellula	U - 0244	Self	—	One Control Test 3.
Jul. 1025	28	Lancaster III	N D 743	Self	4 Crew	Stick Forces per G with bomb load.

The pilots at RAE Farnborough had an extraordinarily varied workload. On 26 July 1944, Eric Brown flew a Lancaster III, Seafire IIC, Spitfire VA, Firebrand and finally 'stepped out' of his Tempest V.

'I finally stepped out at 1,200 ft'

Michael Turner '14

The pond that received my unexpected visit was shallow and not particularly fragrant, so I moved as smartly as I could to the bank, only to find myself face to face with the only other occupant of the field – a very large and unfriendly looking bull. As I moved a few steps closer it lowered its head and snorted through its nose. Discretion being the better part of valour, I did a smart about turn and headed for the opposite bank, but just as I reached dry land I realised I had been beaten to it by my bovine acquaintance, who was determined to provide a personal reception service. There was nothing for it but to await deliverance in some form or other.

Alerted by the exploding aircraft, the local fire brigade and police soon arrived, but baulked at the site of the bull. There was a hiatus while the police went in search of the farmer, who eventually appeared with a short rope which he passed through the animal's nose ring and then gently led him away like a pet poodle. I may be wrong, but I could swear that bull winked at me as he departed.

Parked at Farnborough, JN735, the Tempest V Eric Brown 'stepped out of' at 1,200 ft.

'There was nothing for it but to await deliverance in some form or other.'

Caught in the crossfire

Flying a magnificent fighter compensated for double trouble

5 May 1945

Caught in the crossfire

Flying a magnificent fighter compensated for double trouble

When Nazi Germany was crumbling to a final collapse, I flew an Avro Anson with a co-pilot and three boffins from RAE Farnborough to Husum Airfield on the west coast of Schleswig Holstein, where the British 2nd Army had alerted us to their discovery of a Wing of Messerschmitt Me 163B rocket fighters. We spent the evening of 3 May 1945 and the morning of the next day examining these and making arrangements to have them guarded until our return. While there, we discovered that there was another cache of wonderful war prizes, both piston- and jet-engined aircraft. They were at a large nightfighter base at Grove, located towards the north of Denmark. This was very exciting news, but we were deeply concerned that the retreating Germans might vandalise them if we did not get there straight away.

The 2nd Army was convinced that its boys were already on their way and would surely be there, and in control, by the time we arrived, so shortly after midday we set off for Grove. We arrived there mid-afternoon and from the air could not see any sign of the 2nd Army. It all looked peaceful, so I decided to land. We touched down, taxied to the control tower and shut down the engines. The only people that approached us were a small group of three Germans led by an officer wearing a sword. When I got out of the aircraft he saluted me and announced in German that he was a Lieutenant-Colonel in charge. I could see he wore the insignia of a major, and asked where the senior officers were, because it was such a large base. He replied that they had departed a day earlier and left him in charge, and then offered me his sword in surrender.

Left: The flight path taken by Eric Brown (in blue) and the route of the advancing 2nd Army (in red).

Schleswig became the main gathering point for the RAE's collection of captured German aircraft.

Above: The 2nd Army had skirted Flensburg to avoid a direct confrontation with the crack SS regiment guarding members of the new German Government. A number of leading officials, including

General Jodl, were eventually captured in the village of Muivik, a few miles from Flensburg, by the 1st Battalion, The Cheshire Regiment. (© Imperial War Museums BU 6695)

Left: Josef 'Pips' Priller, was a German ace and commander of Jagdgeschwader 26 who were equipped with Fw 190s from 1941 onwards. During his extraordinary combat career, flying 1,307 missions, he had achieved 101 victories. It was his personal Fw 190D-9, Werk-Nr. 211016 (nicknamed Jutta) which Eric requisitioned at Grove.

Above: At the beginning of 1945, having reached the rank of Geschwader-kommodore, Joseph Priller was appointed Inspekteur der Jagdflieger Ost, putting an end to his operational flying career.

I estimated there must be some 3,000 Germans on this base, and asked to be shown what aircraft they had. It was a mouthwatering selection, with Ju 188s, He 219s, Arado 234B jets and a solitary Focke-Wulf Fw 190D-9, which had been for the sole use of the base commander. I then asked where my small team could be accommodated, and he offered us the base commander's quarters on the airfield. Any port in a storm until the 2nd Army arrived.

The quarters were well equipped and there was food available, but we were uneasy about the situation and did not know what the night might bring. At about 22:00 on this balmy spring evening there was suddenly a cacophony of noise and a great deal of shouting. We drew our pistols in readiness to defend ourselves when a stream of civilians, the local population of Grove village, appeared, all carrying bottles

Above: During 1945 hundreds of captured enemy aircraft, including these Fw 190s, were gathered at airfields in Northern Germany. Some were forwarded to various Allied forces for flight testing; the remainder were destroyed on the ground. (© Imperial War Museums CL 3307)

Right: The iconic Fw 190D-9, which Eric Brown has described as one of the best fighters of WWII. He was particularly grateful for its outstanding turn of speed in his hasty escape from Flensburg.

Below: The elegant Fw 190D with its extended nose and additional supercharger air intake, was the obvious precursor of Kurt Tank's later TA 152.

Shown here is Fw 190 V53, Werk-Nr. 170003, a converted Fw 190A-7 airframe that as the Fw 190D-0 became the first evaluation aircraft for the Fw 190D series.

of aquavit which they had kept hidden from the Germans throughout the war. They ringed themselves three deep around the house and sang themselves into a drunken stupor. We didn't get much sleep, but did not mind as long as they formed our Danish line of defence.

Next morning the advance party of the 2nd Army arrived and briefed me that they had been held up by the situation at Flensburg near the Danish border, where Grand Admiral Dönitz,

'I was being fired on by both the British and German forces, so I rammed on full throttle and was away like a scalded cat.'

Left: The entry in Eric Brown's log book describing his close encounter at Flensburg. It also illustrates the hectic nature of his time in Germany, by 18:00 hours the same day, he was again in the cockpit carrying out handling tests on the Me 262B-1a/U1 jet fighter.

Year 1944		AIRCRAFT		Pilot, or 1st Pilot	2nd Pilot, Pupil or Passenger	DUTY (Including Results and Remarks)
Month	Date	Type	No.			
----	—	—	—	—	—	— Totals Brought Forward
Dec. 1050	22	S.M.95	41003	Self	2 Crew	Handling at Vergiate.
1945						
Mar. 1130	4	Sikorsky R-4B	KL	Self	—	Speke to Farnborough incl. first solo.
May 1035	5	Fw.190D-9	211016	Self	—	Grove to Flensburg and Schleswig. Made a touch down at Flensburg but was fired
May 1200	5	Me.262B-1a/U1	110305	Self	—	Handling at Schleswig. two-seater.
May 1205	6	Do.17Z		Self	F/O. Sullivan	Lübeck to Schleswig. Handling en route

Once back at Farnborough, the Fw 190 was extensively flight-tested by Eric Brown and the other pilots of RAE's Flight Section. Here he is flying a Fw 190A-4, PE882, in formation with Seafire VB R7195, during a tour to show the German fighter at various airfields around the UK.

Hitler's successor after the Führer's suicide in the Berlin bunker, was holed-up with his staff and protected by a crack regiment of the SS.

With this knowledge, I decided to leave my team behind and set out to find a suitable airfield to act as the RAE base for our rapidly mounting collection of captured enemy aircraft.

On the way up to Grove I had spotted a possible candidate at Schleswig, so decided to head there. I therefore had the Germans prepare the Fw 190D-9 for flight, and by late morning was airborne and heading south. I was very impressed by this latest product from the Focke-Wulf stable, and was soon to have reason to be even

more impressed. My route to Schleswig would take me very close to Flensburg, where my map showed me there was an airfield in the near vicinity, and which my 2nd Army friends at Grove assured me would be in British hands. It seemed sensible to drop in and see how things were going. I set up my final approach, but suddenly, just as I touched down, a hailstorm of tracer erupted from either side of the airfield. I was being fired on by both the British and German forces, so I rammed on full throttle and was away like a scalded cat. Luckily the 190 was one of the Luftwaffe's fastest fighters and had a wonderful rate of climb, so the speed of my departure made me a difficult target, and I heaved a sigh of relief as I passed out of range. I finally reached the safety of Schleswig Airfield, which was firmly in British hands and was to become the RAE base for the next year.

Later at Schleswig I had time to conduct proper flight trials on the Fw 190D-9, and rated it the second-best wartime piston-engine fighter I ever flew. It was behind the Spitfire XIV, but just by a whisker!

Fw 190A-4/U8 PP882, being flown by Eric Brown during tests by RAE Farnborough. In his final appraisal of the Fw 190 he wrote: 'A superb fighter with outstanding rate of roll, the Dora or D-9 version is German fighter technology at its best'.

Finding a Siebel in a haystack

My trusty German Siebel Si 204 knew the meaning of 'any port in a storm'

22 August 1945

Finding a Siebel in a haystack

My trusty German Siebel Si 204 knew the meaning of 'any port in a storm'

During my hectic nine months with the Farren Mission in 1945, scouring the Third Reich for any vestiges of Germany's advanced aviation technology, I was assigned two aircraft for my own personal use – Bell Airacobra AH574, from RAE Farnborough's stable, and a Siebel Si 204D liberated from the Luftwaffe. Both proved invaluable.

The Si 204D was a twin-engined transport aircraft carrying two crew and up to five passengers with accompanying baggage. I utilised this aircraft extensively, and it gave yeoman service and proved itself an excellent utilitarian machine totally suited to my purpose. A tailwheel aircraft, it had a wingspan of 70 ft and was powered by two 600 hp air-cooled Argus engines turning two-bladed propellers. It had a wonderful cockpit with an excellent view from its all-glazed nose.

Eric Brown's Bell Airacobra, AH574, achieving its own place in aviation history when he landed it on HMS Pretoria Castle, *the first deck landing of a tricycle undercarriaged aircraft on a British aircraft carrier.*

I transported many of Britain's top scientists on these exploratory sorties, which we had to make quite frequently, often to remote destinations. On one such occasion on 22 August 1945, while ferrying four eminent boffins en route to Norway, the Siebel's port engine began to misfire. Checking the map, my co-pilot identified a deserted airstrip at Bad Oeynhausen, where we decided to put down. On approach at 100 ft with wheels and flaps lowered I suddenly saw a tractor crossing the single tarmac runway. This was of course, an illegal activity, life in post-war occupied Germany was heavily regulated by the Allies. All runways were out of bounds to everyone except military personnel and local agriculture was strictly limited to the outer perimeters of airfields.

I had no option but to open up the engines to full power to go round again for a second

Above: The extensively glazed cockpit gave a superb all-round view and the two 600 hp Argus As 411 12-cylinder engines were normally very reliable. All-in-all it was the ideal aircraft for our task.

Left: Eric Brown's log book for 22 August 1945. After their 90 minute unscheduled stop at Bad Oeynhausen, they continued on to Fassberg.

Aug. 1440	21	Si.204D	221558	Self	2 Crew, 4 Passengers	Farnborough to Coxyde (Belgium) Forced down by front. Aerodrome deserted
Aug. 1840	21	Si.204D	221558	Self	2 Crew, 4 Passengers	Coxyde to Valkenburg (Holland). Through thunder and lightning storm.
Aug. 1830	22	Si.204D	221558	Self	2 Crew, 4 Passengers	Valkenburg to Bad Oeynhausen. Landed at deserted air-strip with ropey port engine which packed up on going round again with everything down. Parked in wheat field without any damage. Carried out later.
Aug. 1300	22	Si.204D	221558	Self	2 Crew, 4 Passengers	Bad Oeynhausen to Fassberg (Germany).
Aug. 1635	22	Si.204D	221558	Self	2 Crew, 4 Passengers	Fassberg to Holtenau (Kiel).
Aug. 1120	23	Si.204D	221558	Self	2 Crew, 2 Passengers	Holtenau to Schleswig. Pouring rain.
Aug. 1500	23	Si.204D	221558	Self	2 Crew, 2 Passengers	Schleswig to Flensburg (Germany).

The trusty Siebel 204D AM28, (originally Werk-Nr 221558) which became my personal mode of transport while I scoured the remnants of the German Third Reich in search of the Luftwaffe's more exciting aircraft.

attempt to land, when suddenly the port engine again coughed badly and began to lose power. The runway was very short with rising ground ahead, and at 50 ft over the threshold I realised that the point of no return had been reached. The airfield was being cultivated and there were haystacks dotted all around, so I eased off the corrective right rudder I had applied, let the Siebel drift on to the grass and headed it full-tilt into a haystack. The windmilling propellers acted as threshing machines and we decelerated smartly but without damage.

The offending farmer fled on his tractor, leaving my illustrious passengers to defluff the straw from the wings, while my German mechanic and I removed the oiled-up spark plugs from the Argus engine and cleaned them with the aid of our passenger's pipecleaners and nail files. We all then pushed on the leading edge of the wings to get the Siebel clear of the haystack, enough to start the engines and thoroughly run them up before re-embarking and taking off with somewhat bated breath.

After that incident I have often reflected on what might have occurred if I had attempted

Michael Turner
'14

to fly out of the initial situation. We would almost certainly have hit the rising ground ahead with the inevitably disastrous results. Two of my four passengers were the Head of the Naval Aircraft Department, Lewis Boddington, and his deputy, Dr J Thomlinson. These two were subsequently to be responsible for many brilliant ideas in carrier aviation, including the angled deck. This alone completely revolutionised aircraft carrier operations and led us on the path to the giant vessels of today and their supersonic aircraft. The cost of losing these two outstanding scientists would have been inestimable.

I can never reminisce about the Si 204D without reflecting on the strange but loyal friendship I experienced with the two German crew members who accompanied me on our many flights to outposts of the Third Reich. I first met them during a pre-Siebel trip to Sola Airfield at Stavangar in Norway, to investigate a reported batch of Arado Ar 234B jets which were eventually ferried to RAE Farnborough. On this occasion, I was so impressed by the

knowledge shown by these two Luftwaffe prisoners of war – Walter Rautenberg, an engine fitter, and Walter Renner, an electronics technician – that I had them released from the PoW cage and offered them the opportunity to work under my supervision, both in Germany and at RAE Farnborough. This they accepted readily, and stayed with me until they were repatriated to Germany in 1947. Both proved invaluable and provided a wealth of experience and guidance on maintaining our captured German aircraft, and we remained firm friends until their deaths.

Eric Brown and Lewis Boddington pace HMS Warrior's *temporary flexible deck, shortly before Boddington's development of the angled deck was tested on HMS* Triumph *in February 1952.*

Emergency stop!

Jet engine explosion
terminates my first flight
in an Arado Ar 234B

24 June 1945

Emergency stop!

Jet engine explosion prematurely terminates my first flight in an Arado Ar 234B

On 4 May 1945 I had found a number of Arado 234B jet bomber/reconnaissance aircraft at the Luftwaffe airfield at Grove, about two-thirds of the way up Denmark. The airfield fell into our hands, but the war was still active and, rather than test-flying the Arado, my priority was to select an RAE staging base in Schleswig Holstein where the British 2nd Army were in control. Eventually the choice fell on Schleswig Airfield, which then became my main operating base in post-war Germany.

After a spell of hectic activity both at Farnborough and in Germany, including flying

This Ar 234B-1/b, Werk-Nr 140 312, was taken to Wright Field, Ohio, in 1945 for evaluation. It was allegedly captured at Saalbach Airfield and was on the strength of 1./FAGr.110, performing reconnaissance missions during the closing months of the war in Europe.

An Arado Ar 234B-2 Blitz is refuelled by Luftwaffe PoWs at the Danish airfield of Grove, Jutland, before being ferried to Schleswig on route to RAE Farnborough.

the Me 262 twin-jet fighter and the Me 163B rocket fighter, my thoughts turned again to the Ar 234B. This was powered by two axial-flow jet engines of the same type as those fitted to the Me 262, and I was aware that these Jumo 004 engines had a scrap life of only 25 hours. By this time I also knew from experience that the Germans were meticulous about destroying the service records of all aircraft before capture, and that we would get no help from Luftwaffe aircrew, but a varying degree of assistance from groundcrew.

However, I had managed to cope so far, so set off from Schleswig for Grove on 24 June 1945, full of anticipatory interest at the chance of flying this beautifully streamlined single-seat aeroplane, which was reputed to be faster than any Allied fighter and so did not carry any defensive armament.

Eric Brown climbs into the cockpit of one of the Ar 234Bs which were brought back to Britain for flight testing in the immediate post-war period. (RAF Museum Hendon P000425)

Refuelling an Arado at Farnborough. The two German PoWs in the photograph are Walter Renner, an electronics technician, working in the cockpit, and Walter Rautenberg, an engine fitter standing to the right. These men provided invaluable help and expertise to Eric Brown, and became his life-long friends. (RAF Museum Hendon P000426)

Since neither I nor my accompanying boffins knew anything much about the mechanical innards of the Ar 234B, we had arranged for Luftwaffe groundcrew to service it before our arrival. So in mid-afternoon I clambered into the almost helicopter-like Plexiglas cockpit and settled myself to get acquainted with the layout. When satisfied, I started up the engines, waved the chocks away and got going. I taxied out to the duty runway, lined up for take-off and slowly opened the throttles. After 15 seconds I eased my feet off the brake pedals, and just as I began to feel the surge of power the Ar 234B was known to deliver, there was a tremendous explosion in the starboard engine. Bits of shattered metal and turbine blades tore into the fuselage just behind the cockpit, and a large hole appeared in the starboard wing above the jagged remains of the engine.

Michael Turner
'14

Photographed after its arrival at RAE Farnborough, this is one of nine Ar 234Bs flown to the UK for detailed evaluation and flight testing.

The aircraft lurched forward and I hit the brakes, luckily bringing it to a halt within a few yards. Needless to say, one's immediate concern in these situations is the danger of a fuel leak, so I rapidly shut down the port engine and left the cockpit like a 'scalded cat'.

After this episode there was the inevitable post-mortem as to the cause, and some of my team suspected sabotage by a member of the maintenance crew. In hindsight, I am more inclined to put it down to the failed engine probably having approached, or exceeded its limited 25 hour life before it gave up.

Throughout my time in Germany, the majority of captured groundcrew gave me nothing but help and support and were completely trustworthy. I subsequently flew Jumo 004 engines for some 100 hours without any serious trouble.

'Bits of shattered metal and turbine blades tore into the fuselage just behind the cockpit ...'

The Junkers Jumo 004 B-1 powered both the Ar 234B and the Me 262. This example, designated M-04, was built in post-war Czechoslovakia.

A maverick glider with a killer streak

Testing the deadly General Aircraft GAL.56

24 July 1946

A maverick glider with a killer streak

Testing the deadly General Aircraft GAL.56

Possibly the most difficult, probably one of the worst, and certainly among the most dangerous aircraft I have ever flown.

The end of World War II unleashed a torrent of innovatory developments in aviation following the revelation of the startling technical advances made for the German Luftwaffe. Great Britain reacted like the other former allies and sought to grab these opportunities by building experimental prototypes incorporating new aerodynamic or engineering ideas. General Aircraft was one British company to get a government contract to build three experimental gliders with varying degrees of sweepback on an all-wing semi-tailless design.

The GAL.56 was the prime aircraft of the three to be chosen for full-scale testing. Before moving to that phase it was subjected to intensive windtunnel testing which revealed some tricky characteristics. The GAL.56/01 'Medium V' had 28 degrees of sweepback on its wings, at the extremities of which were fins and rudders. It carried two crew sitting in tandem. It was a large ungainly looking aircraft with an undercarriage of substantial proportions and oversize wheels that did nothing to improve its appearance.

Because of its windtunnel prognosis it was decided to dump it in the lap of RAE Farnborough, where it arrived in the spring of 1946, labelled as a problem child, which was certainly no exaggeration. Anyway, it became my assignment, and so the battle of wits with this capricious creature began for me on 1 May 1946.

All flights were to be made with the glider towed by a Spitfire LF IX to 20,000 ft for release and subsequent testing on the glide back to base. Right away take-off was a tricky procedure, the whole problem being caused by the violent ground effect to which the aircraft was subject, for the cushion of air between the wings and the runway gave a strong nose-up change of trim. Thus on take-off the loss of ground effect would cause it to dart sharply back into the ground, and no amount of

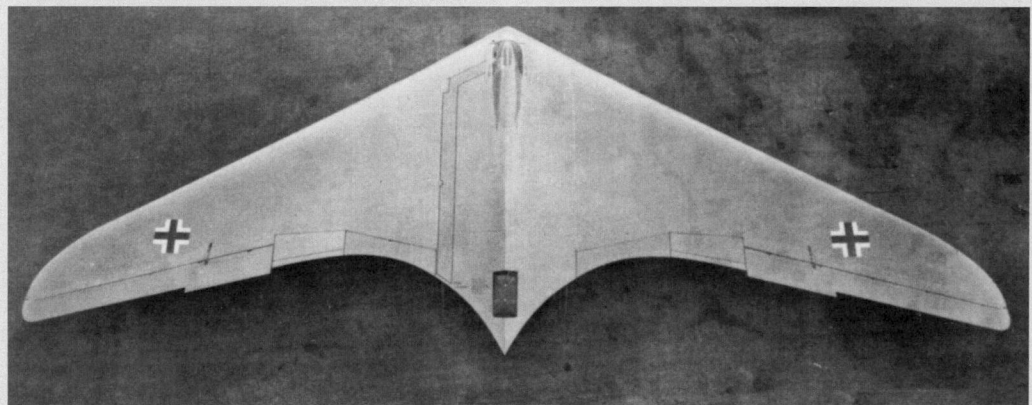

The Horten IX prototype. During the closing months of the war there had been rumours about the work of the Horten brothers and their experiments with all-wing aircraft. Their revolutionary prototypes were eventually captured at Saalbach in 1945. Their discovery gave birth to a number of experimental all-wing and delta-winged aircraft. The GAL.56 was one example, and the design of de Havilland Aircraft's infamous DH 108 was also heavily influenced by the new German data reaching Britain at the end of the war.

Far left: TS507, the Medium V version, had a 33.5-degree wing sweepback. Robert Kronfeld piloted it on its maiden flight on 13 November 1944 at Farnborough, towed by an Armstrong Whitworth Whitley.

Left & below: The Maximum V version had a 40-degree wing sweepback. Wingspan was the same as that of the GAL.56/01. Its first flight took place on 30 May 1946.

backward elevator would prevent this at speeds up 80 mph. Now I understood the need for the outsize landing gear.

On tow the glider was very pleasant to fly unless the tug's slipstream was inadvertently entered, when all longitudinal and directional control was lost until the glider was eventually tossed clear after a severe pounding.

In free flight the GAL.56 was very stable longitudinally at forward centre of gravity (c.g.), then stability fell off as the c.g. moved aft. This behaviour I have found usual with all-wing aircraft.

The internal structure of the GAL's wing and fuselage was made entirely of wood, with a wood-paper skin covering.

The General Aircraft workshop with the GAL.56 approaching completion in the foreground. At the rear are Sikorsky R4 Hoverfly helicopters being modified for Service use. The company later merged with Blackburn Aircraft and moved to Brough Aerodrome, Yorkshire.

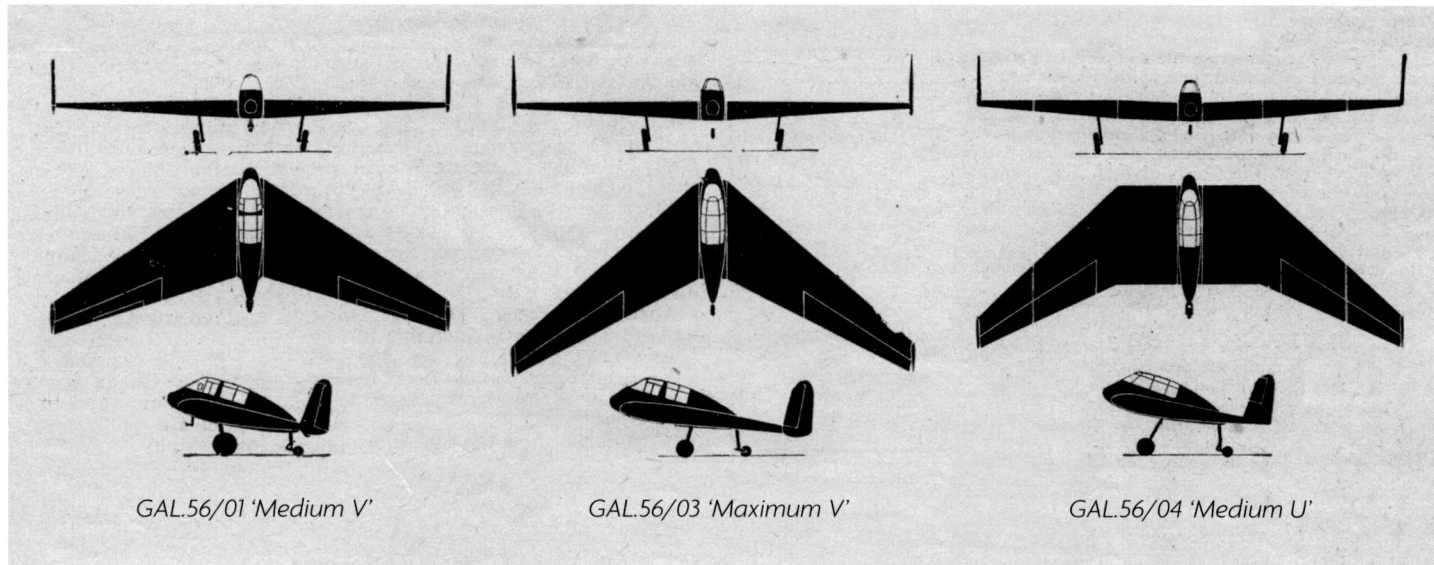

General arrangement drawings of the three variations of the GAL. 56, highlighting the different wing configurations.

GAL.56/01 'Medium V' GAL.56/03 'Maximum V' GAL.56/04 'Medium U'

Then I moved on to the stalling tests, which revealed very unusual characteristics, so much so that it was decided to have both wings fitted with wool tufts to show the airflow patterns, which were recorded by an auto-observer. This was a rudimentary forerunner of the modern black box giving information on airspeed and control movements.

On 26 July 1946 I took the GAL up again, accompanied by one of our intrepid Flight Observers, Miss Curtiss. I carried out a number of manoeuvres and then moved on to the stall. As we approached it, a nose-up pitching moment started showing itself and developed into a definite self-stalling tendency, which rapidly increased in backward force and movement of the control wheel which I could not overpower. When the control wheel was getting near the back stop and the airspeed had dropped to 55 mph a tail slide developed, and having been warned by our boffins not to try and manoeuvre out of this situation by

Michael Turner '14

The extraordinary bug-shaped profile of TS507, the GAL.56/01 'Medium V'.

using lateral elevon, I sat tight for a few seconds until it felt as if the aircraft was going over on its back. At this stage I pushed the wheel hard forward until a force of some 60 lb was applied, when it met an aerodynamic stop caused by the build-up in control force. The glider then paused, the nose dropped violently until it was level with the horizon, paused again, and abruptly fell into a steep dive before control was regained. Because of developing cloud cover we barely made it back, just stalling in over the hedge at the end of the runway. The GAL with its infamous stall characteristics pitched forwards coming to rest on its nose. At which point Miss Curtiss was, perhaps understandably, violently ill, all over the interior of the cockpit. Normally the ground crew would charge the culprit a fee for cleaning up, but such was the reputation of the GAL they instantly waived it.

I conducted some twenty flights, each including a stall/tail slide, with the help of our stalwart group of flight test observers. They were understandably less than enthusiastic for the assignment and none of them volunteered more than once. Their reluctance was probably exacerbated by the fact that even the arrival back at base, after our hair-raising adventures, was fraught with potential danger.

I am certainly of the view that the GAL.56 was the most difficult aircraft I have ever experienced. Although a normal approach was always made and then a normal hold-off attempted, it usually managed to coincide with

The Medium V, TS507 being towed by a Halifax at Lasham Airfield.

the onset of the inevitable ground effect. The subsequent nose-up pitch usually led to a display of the aircraft's peculiar stalling behaviour about 3ft off the ground. The resulting dive into the runway inevitably produced an enormous bounce from the non-resilient undercarriage, plus an instinctive pull-back on the control wheel, to start the sequence off all over again.

As can be imagined, flying the GAL.56 was not recommended as a form of relaxation, so it was with a feeling of relief that the test programme was successfully concluded on

Just scraped in! Eric Brown's log book entry for the flight with Miss Curtiss and its unconventional ending.

A cutting from the Daily Express, the day after Kronfeld's death, with a diagram showing the sequence of events leading up to the fatal crash.

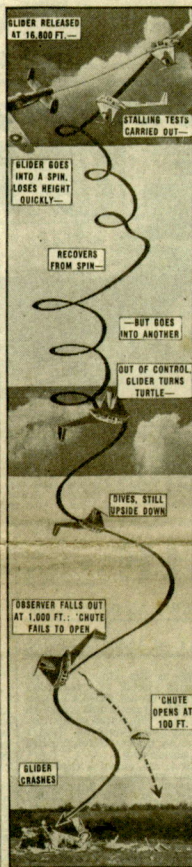

28 August 1947, when I flew the glider to Lasham Airfield, near Basingstoke. There I handed it over to Robert Kronfeld, the General Aircraft chief test pilot, who was going to repeat some of the RAE tests for his own experience.

Robert Kronfeld was an Austrian glider pilot who had built up a reputation for his skill in the 1920s. As a Jew he was prohibited from flying in 1933 by the new Nazi government, so fled Germany back to Austria and then on to England, where he settled in 1938. In 1939 he became a British citizen and served in the RAF, eventually being posted to the Airborne Forces Experimental Establishment on military glider development. Kronfeld flew the GAL.56 spasmodically for some six months, and was involved in stalling tests when on 12 February 1948 he was killed at the age of 43 when the aircraft entered an inverted dive, although his flight observer baled out successfully. I was greatly saddened by this news, but it did not surprise me, for I had always had the instinctive feeling that the GAL.56 would one day win the eternal battle of wits with those who flew it.

The eye of the storm

The Faustian hell of flight in a thunderhead

9 July 1947

The eye of the storm

The Faustian hell of flight in a thunderhead

In the immediate post-WWII era the emphasis on aviation development switched from military to civil, as airlines sprung into renewed action and wanted new airliners. At first this demand had to be met by adapting military bombers and transport aircraft such as the Avro Lincoln, Short Stirling and Vickers Warwick, but these did not provide the passenger comfort or payload required by burgeoning airlines.

One area of concern that had to be addressed was that of structural integrity in bad weather conditions, especially in the tropics, where monsoons created cloud formations containing violent air currents and atmospheric conditions that were both structurally dangerous and hazardous for sustained flight control. Superimposed on all this was the fact that aviation was entering the jet age and

Opposite: Test flights to explore the effects of flying in cumulo-nimbus and storm clouds became necessary with the post-war expansion in civil aviation. Studying the stresses encountered was vital to ensure the safety and structural integrity of early airliners such as (top) the Vickers Warwick and (below) the Short Stirling, both conversions from military bombers.

Below: The Spitfire LF IX was chosen for the tests because of the strength of its airframe.

Eric's 'office' for the 55-minute test flight, only dimly lit by the cockpit lights. Huge discharges of electricity from the lightning, and the severe turbulence, caused the instruments to behave erratically. The only reliable information came from the artificial horizon.

emphasis would change from low-level air turbulence to high-altitude clear-air turbulence and towering thunderheads

At the RAE we had for years been doing high-altitude flights daily in a pressure cabin Spitfire XIX, looking for clear-air turbulence usually associated with jetstream activity. It was now decided to investigate severe turbulence by penetrating the anvil-shaped apex of a towering thunderhead, using a Spitfire LF IX because of its highly stressed structure.

This test was very much a waiting game until the right thunderhead appeared, rather like waiting for an enemy alert in the Battle of Britain, then jumping into the Spitfire and heading for the darkest part of the anvil-shaped cloud, somewhere above 30,000 ft. Before entering the utter blackness of the cumulo-nimbus cloud it was essential to switch on the cockpit lighting

The distinctive hammerhead formation of a cumulo-nimbus cloud, which can reach more than 30,000 ft in height. Tremendous forces sometimes in excess of 8 'g' are generated by the rapidly moving air currents within them. These fluctuating forces have destroyed hundreds of aircraft, causing them to break up in mid-air. (© HMSO & Queen's Printer, courtesy of Matthew Clark)

My confidence in the ruggedness of the Spitfire certainly eased what felt like the longest 30 minutes of my life.

rather than fumble for it in the ensuing chaos, as all hell was about to break loose.

The main task now was trying to control the aeroplane on instruments which were all gyrating wildly in the severe turbulence. I soon learned that the golden rule was to concentrate on the artificial horizon and keep the aircraft laterally level without worrying about speed or height, which varied alarmingly as one passed through the thunder cell. These thunder cells were raging cauldrons of noise and light, the noise coming from the thunder and from the hailstones battering the metal skin of the aeroplane, and the light from the lightning which often struck the aircraft. But worst of all was the brilliance, which blinded me each time, so that for a few vital seconds I was unable to read the cockpit instruments.

My Spitfire suffered extensive damage from

Michael Turner '14

hailstones and lightning strikes, and several times the engine cut due to icing. Whenever it was struck by lightning there was a horrible acrid smell like fire and brimstone. St Elmo's fire would glitter round the cockpit rim and circle the spinning airscrew tips with an unearthly sparkle, while inside the cockpit it was as black as night.

I am not going to pretend I was not hugely relieved finally to be spewed out of this thunderhead in one piece, thanks to my sturdy Spitfire, and not, as often happened to lighter aircraft, as confetti.

Jul.	7	1135	1200	Self	—	Inverted Flying.	Spitfire L.F.IX	NH403
Jul.	7	1650	1700	Self		Air Test.	Hoverfly	KA109
Jul.	9	1455	1550	Self	—	Cumulo-Nimbus Cloud Investigation.	Spitfire L.F.IX	NH403
Jul.	9	1615	1630	Self		Air Test.	Hoverfly	KA109
Jul.	11	1030	1345	Self	—	Farnborough to Gosport and Return.	Avenger III	KE436
Jul.	11	1555	1600	Self	—	Demonstration Catapult Launch for Admiralty and M.O.S. works	Firefly IV	TW735

Above: Not an extensive entry for what seemed like a visit to Hell and back.

Top: The Spitfire LF IX was fitted with strain gauges, but they were the only forms of data recording available.

The bulk of the information gathered came from Eric's evaluation and personal experiences during the flight.

Wings flapping

Fatigue can cripple machines as well as humans

October 1944

Wings flapping

Fatigue can cripple machines as well as humans

I have witnessed some weird and alarming incidents during aircraft carrier operations. One I remember well was a Fairey Firefly, the last one of a whole carrier group to touch down. It bounded over both safety barriers to smash into a full deck park of Sea Furies and Fireflies, whose ground crews were assisting the aircrews to leave their aircraft. The resultant carnage was a horror to witness. More routinely I have seen arrester hooks fail, arrester wires snap and undercarriages collapse, all due to repeated metallurgical overstressing, causing fatigue failure.

A rather unusual case of such a failure occurred to me in a Lease-Lend Grumman Avenger at RAE Farnborough in 1944. We were carrying out trials of a new hydraulic-pneumatic catapult using the American tail-down method of launching, which did not require the use of a

The sturdy lines of the Grumman TBM-1C Avenger owed much to the design of its smaller Wildcat ancestor.

Its strength and reliability made it popular with carrier pilots, both British and American.

Below: An Avenger with wings folded, revealing the sturdy undercarriage which survived many a hard carrier deck landing. It also managed to absorb Eric's impact of some 16 ft/sec.

Bottom: The deck landing sequence of an Avenger, highlighting the speed with which the wings could be folded and the flight deck cleared in readiness for the next aircraft.

trolley. The aircraft had one or two hooks positioned near the centre section, and to these were attached a single or twin bridles leading down to a shuttle or pair of shuttles in the accelerator tracks. The tail was fitted with a holdback unit incorporating a retaining ring which snapped to release the aircraft at a predetermined pressure as the catapult fired.

I had carried out dozens of accelerator launches and was expecting the usual sharp jerk, smooth run down the track and then lift-off. Well, the aircraft was shot off so violently at 2.5 'g', that the engine cut and the Avenger's wings started to fold back. By the end of the track they were flopping loosely like a wounded

Michael Turner '14

bird and I was projected into the air to a height of about 15ft before dropping like a stone. As I fell back to earth I pulled back optimistically on the elevator so that the Avenger hit the ground only slightly nose-down, and the extraordinarily sturdy Grumman undercarriage absorbed an estimated vertical velocity of 16ft/sec without damage. However, the post-accident analysis showed that the Grumman wing-locking bolts were not made of the same stern stuff, but despite this the fault really lay with the acceleration characteristics of the catapult.

This new type of catapult was designed to give much higher velocities than 2.5'g', so we started a series of tests to smooth out the acceleration curve. These tests involved frequent engine cut-outs due to temporary fuel starvation, but we eventually got such good results that we were able to go up to 4.6'g' – a record of some sort.

The Institute of Aviation Medicine based at Farnborough began to take an interest in the physiological effects of such high 'g' launchings. As part of their investigations they decided to enlist the active help of my ever-present Norwegian Elkhound, Chuck, to see the effect of 'g' on a creature whose heart lay, unlike a human being's, in the horizontal plane. He collapsed instantly on the floor of the Avenger, but got so fond of aiding science that for a long time after these tests he continued to turn up at the site, hoping that he would be needed and that the attendant fuss would be made of him.

Above left: The Avenger was heavily involved in the European and Pacific campaigns and played an important role in most of the major battles.

Above: Chuck, my faithful Elkhound, who was so eager to help the Institute of Aviation Medicine in its research on high 'g' launches

Not a good day at work. The engine cut due to fuel starvation on the first attempt at just 2.5'g'. Then the wing-locking bolts failed, resulting in a bone-jarring landing at about 16 ft/sec. The third attempt also nearly ended in failure as the tailwheel was damaged when it struck the shuttle, causing Eric to hit his chest on the chart board.

Oct. 1040	24	Seafire XV	PR 556	Self	—	Farnborough to Blackbushe.
Oct. 800	25	Meteor III	EE 476	Self	—	Effect of Dive Brakes on Deck-Landing Approach Conditions.
Oct. 1910	25	Avenger	JZ 298	Self	—	B.H.V Accelerator Proofing. Initial launch at 2.5g (54 knots). Level grundir show. Engine cut due to fuel starvation, and wings unlocked due to vibration when about to launch. On second attempt the tail wheel struck the towing shuttle doing slight damage, and the chart board struck me in the chest under 'g' effect. Flare path landing.
Oct. 1135	28	Avenger	JZ 298	Self	—	B.H.V Accelerator Proofing up to 2.7g. Very violent. 5 A.T.O a
Oct. 1125	29	Avenger	JZ 298	Self	—	B.H.V Accelerator Proofing. Dis. 2700 yds. 2.6g. 9 A.T.O a

Avenger Mk III KE436, primed and ready on the BH.5 catapult. Eric Brown was personally responsible for the high 'g' launch tests at RAE Farnborough throughout his tenure at Aero Flight. (Farnborough Air Sciences)

Avenger Mk III KE436, with the holdback unit connected to the tailwheel assembly, on the BH.5 catapult at RAE Farnborough. (Farnborough Air Sciences)

On the skids

Once again the
dangerous Me 163B
has the last laugh

November 1947

On the skids

Once again the dangerous Me 163B has the last laugh

The collapse of the Third Reich in 1945 revealed an Aladdin's cave of advanced aviation technology to the Allied victors. I was completely fascinated by one aircraft in particular, their tiny – and lethally dangerous – Me 163B rocket fighter, and had an overwhelming desire to fly it as soon as possible.

Before my only powered flight in the Me 163B at Husum Airfield on 10 June 1945, it was realised that we were dealing with a dangerous aeroplane. This was mainly due to the volatility of its fuels and, particularly, of the concentrated hydrogen peroxide which constituted its primary combustion fluid.

It was obvious that I could not just hop into one and take off, as I had done so many times before, with a minimum of briefing. The approach speed was 145–150 mph, the touchdown speed 125 mph. Landing was done

An Me 163B-1as begins a so-called 'sharp start' at Bad Zwischenahn. For take-off the aircraft was trimmed tail heavy and the wheels were jettisoned at an altitude of 15–30 ft.

A frame from a Nazi propaganda film of the 'Revolutionary new German fighter in flight'.

A pilot climbs into his Komet at Bad Zwischenahn. His one-piece flying suit and overboots are made from a special acid-resistant material which was supposed to protect the occupant from the corrosive T-Stoff in the far from unlikely event of a bad landing – assuming his aircraft did not explode.
(The Aeroplane)

on a skid, the wheeled trolley having been jettisoned on take-off. Another major concern was the composition of the volatile fuel mixture, and its availability.

I went over to the Walter works in Kiel with a team of scientists, where Dr Hellmuth Walter, inventor of the rocket motor used in the Me 163B, put on a demonstration for us. It was a frightening display, weird and futuristic. Immured behind a glass panel nine inches thick, we watched the motor run out on the bench for two minutes. The roar of noise was shattering; the whole place quaked and trembled. All the men taking part in the demonstration were swathed in rubber aprons, gumboots and hats, and looked very Wellsian.

But the simple performance which followed was even more sobering. Dr Walter took two glass rods, on one of which was a droplet of

Below: The original prototype Me 163A (left), in company with its larger and redesigned derivative, the Me 163B.

Right: Dr Hellmuth Walter, inventor of the Walter HWK 509A bi-fuel rocket motor.

concentrated hydrogen peroxide, called T-Stoff, and on the other the same quantity of a solution of hydrazene hydrate in methanol, called C-Stoff. He slowly inclined first one, then the other. A droplet from one rod fell on the floor. A teardrop from the other fell on top of it. There was a violent explosion which blew both rods out of the doctor's hands. After this Faustian exhibition we fully appreciated how dangerous those volatile rocket fuels were.

There were other dangers too, such as incorrectly jettisoning the take-off trolley, which in the case of Hanna Reitsch, the famous German aviatrix, caused her life-threatening injuries. There was also the aircraft's violent behaviour in transonic flight, where, if the critical Mach number of 0.84 was exceeded, it would suddenly tuck under into an extremely steep dive from which there was no recovery.

However, the most common danger was making such a hard touchdown on the landing skid that it caused a serious spinal injury. Such landing contact was further exacerbated if the pilot forgot to return the skid lowering lever to neutral. This rendered the skid rigid under immense hydraulic pressure, removing any shock absorption on touchdown.

With all its problem areas, what was it about the Me 163B that so mesmerised the post-war world of aviation, almost as if she was the mystical siren on the Lorelei Rock in the River Rhine that lured mariners to destruction? I believe the sheer boldness of its innovatory design features were responsible for this reaction.

This same reaction inspired the de Havilland Aircraft Company to embark on the ill-fated DH 108 design. It was also simmering at RAE Farnborough, where two of the captured German aeronautical engineers serving in Aero Flight in 1947 were designing a supersonic research aircraft. They were both well qualified for the task, one being Dr Hans Multhopp, former chief aerodynamicist at Focke-Wulf, and the other,

The cockpit of the Me 163B. The housings running down each side are the lethal T-Stoff fuel tanks. The slightest leak or puncture to either would have proved fatal.

Professor M Winter of the Technical High School at Brunswick, where he was a windtunnel expert.

The Me 163B test programme at RAE began in the late autumn of 1946 and was to be entirely unpowered, as the British authorities had banned the use of T-Stoff in the UK. The Me 163B was towed by a Spitfire IX and was generally limited to a height of 20,000 ft to avoid overheating the Spitfire's engine. Since the Multhopp-Winter proposed aircraft

Michael Turner '14

incorporated a pair of skids for landing at calculated speeds of 160 mph at touchdown, it was decided to initiate a series of landing tests on the Me 163B, starting at speeds of 110 mph and gradually increasing in stages. I had been conducting all Me 163B flights at the Vickers grass airfield at Wisley, adjacent to Farnborough. However, it was felt that this was too tight for the proposed tests, so we transferred to Wittering, a lengthy grass airfield used for emergency landings by crippled bombers during the war. Accordingly I was flown there under tow on 1 November 1947, covering a distance of 120 miles at 3,500 ft.

The Me 163B was at Wittering for almost two weeks while strain gauges were fitted to the landing skid, and I eventually started the trials on 13 November. The landings were to be made without flaps, and my first touchdown speed was 133 mph. The second landing was at 136 mph, and the boffins decided that application of slight flap might prove necessary to get a steeper angle of approach and attain higher touchdown speed without excessive float on hold-off.

'After a run of 610 yards the aircraft came to a standstill just short of the perimeter fence. It took quite a while to cut me free from the wreckage of the cockpit.'

This technique certainly worked, but perhaps was a little too effective. The third landing, on 15 November 1947, gave a touchdown speed of 158 mph. Although actual contact with the ground was not hard, the subsequent run-out was too much for the hydraulic skid, which collapsed and smashed up into the fuselage, ramming the oleo legs through the cockpit floor and jamming the rudder bar fully over to the left. Simultaneously my legs were forced up and jammed beneath the instrument panel. As the Me 163B veered to the left in a gentle curve, which became more pronounced as the left wing dropped and ploughed into the ground, the instrument panel broke loose and peppered me with instruments and associated fittings. After a run of 610 yards the aircraft came to a standstill just short of the perimeter fence.

Right: Hannah Reitsch, committed Nazi and famous German aviatrix, was badly injured when the trolley failed to release and she crashed on take-off while carrying out some early tests on the Me 163B.

Top: The skid assembly as it should have looked. The RAE carried out extensive trials to investigate the performance of the skid landing system.

Above: The skid in the extended landing position.

The damage to the skid is obvious, but the main fuselage remained largely undamaged.

With the mud and debris removed, the damage is clearly visible. The side panels were ripped off in the crash landing.

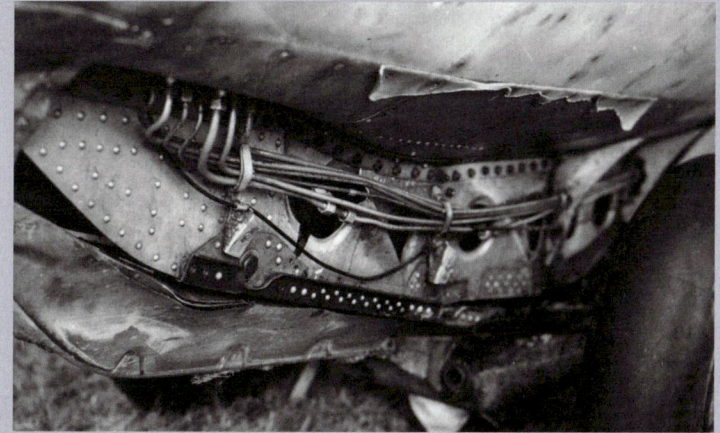

Below: The log entry and photo of the skid after it collapsed on touchdown at 158 mph, '…causing chaos in the cockpit … odds and ends of fittings flying loose'.

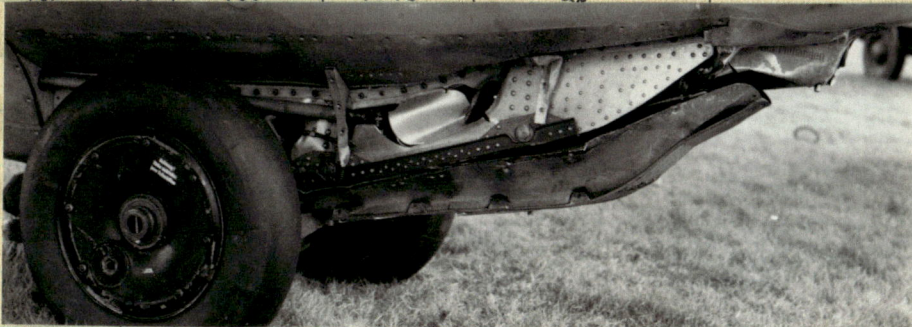

Nov.	13	1420	1635	Self	—	Stability and Control. Fast landing at 219 km/h. (137 mph). Towed to 7,000' by Spitfire L.F.IX. Arrived at dusk very rough & rough ride on T.O.	Me.163B	VF241
Nov.	15	0955	1010	Self	—	Stability and Control. Fast landing at 253 km/h. (158 mph). Had own rough passage on hitting the deck. Skid eventually collapsed under the strain and created chaos in the cockpit. Floor bulged in and jammed rudder bar, camera came completely adrift off its mounting, odds and ends of fittings flying loose and terrific jarring on the old spine. Underside of aircraft a shambles of twisted metal, but otherwise all intact. Self slightly cut, but heavily bruised.	Me.163B	VF241
Nov.	15	1345	1415	Self	1 Crew, 7 Passengers	Wittering to Farnborough.	Viking	VW217
Nov.	17	1140	1555	Self	—	R.A.T.O.G. Proofing of Type. 2 R.A.T.Os.	Sea Fury X	VB857
Nov.	17	1220	1235	Self	Mr. Brotherhood	Loss of Control Investigation.	Hoverfly	KL109
Nov.	17	1440	1510	Self	Mr. Lean	Photography of Wing Tufts on Zaunkönig in Stalled Glides.	Hoverfly	KL109

It took quite a while to cut me free from the wreckage of the cockpit. I had a fair number of cuts and abrasions, and my spine was heavily bruised from its base to the hairline of my neck. Fortunately I had no vertebral damage, as almost always occurred to Me 163B pilots involved in landing accidents.

Great Britain was the only Allied power to carry out flight testing of the Me 163B, which I consider a 'tool of desperation' with an unimpressive operational record. It certainly killed more German than Allied pilots.

Above: The Me 163B VF241, which Eric Brown flew in both towed and gliding flight, the Walter rocket having been removed and an auto-observer inserted in its place.

Right: Eric Brown standing in front of the restored Me 163B VF141 at the RAF Museum, Hendon, more than 50 years after he last flew it.

Below: Eric Brown was invited to attend the unveiling of the German Air Museum's restored Me 163B in July 1965. The airframe had been donated by the RAF in 1964, followed later by a Walter rocket motor discovered in the corner of a shed at Farnborough. Standing alongside him is Rudolf Opitz, who did much of the original flight testing on the Me 163B.

A serial killer that never gave up

The infamous DH 108 claimed the lives of three test pilots

December 1948

A serial killer that never gave up

The infamous DH 108 claimed the lives of three test pilots

An interesting air show photograph of the second, high-speed, prototype of the DH 108 Swallow. The aircraft was built around the fuselage of a de Havilland Vampire, as seen alongside.

Despite all that we knew about the latest German prototypes, no single treasure was seized on with more enthusiasm than the Messerschmitt Me 163B rocket fighter. Great Britain invited selected aircraft manufacturers to visit post-war Germany, and one of the first to take up this offer was the de Havilland Aircraft Company.

The de Havilland design team were deeply intrigued by the Me 163B. They saw great possibilities for its potential development, and lost no time in exploiting this opportunity. Design work began in October 1945 for a swept-back wing, semi-tailless research aircraft. However, their design was powered by a jet engine rather than a rocket motor. At first only two such aircraft were built – a slow-speed version (TG283) with 43° of wing sweep with fixed slots, and a high-speed version (TG306)

with 45° of wing sweep and Handley Page automatic slats which could be locked by the pilot. These prototypes were first flown in May and June 1946 respectively, by Geoffrey de Havilland Jnr.

RAE Farnborough conducted wind-tunnel tests before the first flights and predicted Dutch rolling at low speeds, severe wing dropping in the stall and difficulty in recovery from a spin.

Above left: Geoffrey de Havilland Jnr sinks into the cockpit of the first prototype TG283, for its maiden flight. (BAE SYSTEMS)

Left: The DH 108's maiden take-off from Farnborough on 15 May 1946. (BAE SYSTEMS)

Below: Geoffrey de Havilland was closely involved in all aspects of the development of the DH 108 and was the pilot on its maiden flight. He also became its first victim.

Bottom: John Derry became a test pilot for de Havilland in 1947 and joined the DH 108 test programme. On 6 September 1948 he is thought to have broken the sound barrier in a dive in VW120.

Despite these omens tests went ahead, but disaster struck on 27 September 1946; Geoffrey was killed when TG306 broke up in mid-air while he was conducting transonic speed trials, the intended outcome of which was to be an attempt on the World Speed Record.

In spite of this catastrophe a replacement high-speed version (VW120) was built and first flown in July 1947, but this time fitted with strengthened wings and an ejection seat.

By mid-1947 I had become CO of the prestigious Aerodynamics Flight at RAE Farnborough, and so in early 1948 I was brought into the DH 108 test programme. This was mainly due to my involvement in the RAE testing of the Me 163B and to my experience as the only Allied pilot to have flown it under power. I flew TG283 to Farnborough, where it was re-instrumented before I started a series of stalling tests. These were carried out with the benefit of data compiled in a RAE Report, *Model Spinning Tests on an Experimental Tailless Aircraft (DH 108)*, and with anti-spin parachutes installed in each wingtip.

TG306, the second high-speed prototype, which broke up in mid-air on 27 September 1946, killing Geoffrey de Havilland.

Despite the disastrous crash of TG306, a new high-speed replacement, VW120, the third and final prototype, was completed and had its maiden flight in July 1947.

For our stalling tests a 100ft-long trailing static was fitted, and of course, on RAE advice, there were the wingtip anti-spin parachutes that had been fitted on TG283 from the outset. The trailing static was an extraordinary device, rather like an 11lb practice bomb. It had a perforated spike in the nose, and 100ft of reinforced rubber tubing attached it to the underside of the aircraft. In flight it was released from the cockpit and hung clear of all disturbed airflow, so that a true airspeed was given on a wide-scale indicator in the cockpit and repeated in the automatic observer.

A series of stalls showed a marked tendency to drop the right wing, which then developed into an incipient spin if immediate recovery action was not taken. After this it was decided to go one step further and try to delay the wing drop by the application of a small amount of opposite aileron and moderate rudder. Accordingly, I climbed to 15,000ft and lowered the trailing static before entering the stall, using opposite aileron and rudder as briefed. When the stall came it was a very vicious wing drop to the inverted position, and before I could centralise the rudder, the aircraft was in a steep right-handed inverted spin. Since I had been alerted to this possibility by the RAE report and had been applying left rudder at the stall, I kicked on the rudder with my right foot, but found the somewhat slow rate of rotation was not stopping as quickly as I expected. I pushed harder and then realised the rudder was jammed, probably by the trailing static wound around it. At times of extreme emergency such as this it is amazing how the human body finds unprecedented levels of physical strength, and my herculean push stretched the reinforced

Opposite: The last of the DH 108s to be lost, in May 1950, was TG283. Sqn Ldr 'Jumbo' Genders was conducting stalling tests, and when the aircraft failed to recover he activated the wingtip parachutes, but only one deployed. He tried, unsuccessfully, to bale out, and the aircraft crashed near Hartley Wintney, Hants.

Dec.	6	1110	1115	Self	—	Flexible Deck Landing on "Warrior". 25 m.p.h. over deck, so stepped approach speed up to 123 m.p.h. to give high entry speed into the wire. Arrester gear failed due to maintenance fault and Bottomed to give peak of 5.2g vis it pulled aircraft back 15' No damage!! 3.05g 3.9 W.	Sea Vampire 21	YT 803
Dec.	6	1320	1345	Self	—	"Warrior" to Farnborough. Catapult launch with damaged port wing landing edge. R/T Range Test with ship as fast as heading.	Sea Vampire 21	YT 805
Dec.	6	1445	1510	Self	—	Approach Speed Indicator.	Sea Vampire	TG 314
Dec.	7	1435	1535	Self	4 Crew	Servo Tab Ailerons.	Lancaster III	DS 708
Dec.	8	1035	1120	Self	—	Stalls. Inverted spin with trailing static wound round tail	Swallow	TG 283
Dec.	8	1525	1600	Self	—	Stability and Control.	Swallow	TG 283
Dec.	9	1520	1605	Self	3 Crew	Servo Tab Ailerons.	Lancaster III	DS 708

* AIRBORNE TIME ONLY, <u>NOT</u> TAXYING, TO BE SHOWN.

GRAND TOTAL [Cols. (1) to (8)]
3056 Hrs. 50 Mins.

Totals Carried Forward

Eric Brown's log book covering early December 1948. Having completed landing trials on the experimental flexible deck on HMS Warrior, he returned to RAE Farnborough. On 8 December, while carrying out flight tests, he had the first of his near-fatal incidents in the DH 108, when the static line he was trailing wrapped itself around the fin and rudder while the aircraft was caught in an inverted spin.

Michael Turner '14

The third prototype DH 108 (VW120), is seen here flying from Hatfield on 12 April 1948. Sqn Ldr Stuart Muller-Rowland lost his life flying this aircraft, when it crashed on a test flight on 15 February 1950. (RAF Museum Hendon).

tubing and so eased the rotation until it finally ceased. I was then able to ease the stick back and gently pull through the vertical for a recovery at 3,000 ft. The trailing static was still firmly wrapped around the tail when I landed.

In 1949 the high-speed VW120 was handed over to RAE, and I became heavily involved in the continuing accident investigation into the loss of TG306. This nearly cost me my life on 8 July 1949, when I experienced a runaway divergent longitudinal oscillation in low-level transonic flight. In spite of the flight restrictions imposed on VW120 after this incident, my successor as CO Aero Flight, Sqn Ldr Stuart Muller-Rowland, was killed in the aircraft on 15 February 1950.

During Eric Brown's second near-fatal encounter in the DH 108, when a severe longitudinal oscillation developed at high speed, a pilot flying alongside described what he saw '…as the blur of an unidentifiable machine'. (BAE SYSTEMS)

A DH 108 is wheeled out from its hangar. From the front the distinctive Vampire fuselage is obvious.

Shortly afterwards his successor, Sqn Ldr 'Jumbo' Genders, was carrying out stalling tests on TG283 when he got into a spin and activated the wingtip anti-spin parachutes, but only one opened. He was killed on 1 May 1950.

The dreadful flight record of the DH 108 shook the aviation world and engendered much speculation as to the cause. I was particularly interested because I had not experienced any similar problems when flying the Me 163B. So I consulted the delta and all-wing specialist Alexander Lippisch, who designed the Me 163B, and he was of the opinion that the primary fault with the DH 108 was that its centre of gravity was too far aft. Perhaps the DH 108 was a case of design in haste and repent at leisure.

Cartwheel to disaster

Pulled unconscious from
the sea after crashing the
SR/A1 jet fighter flying boat

August 1949

Cartwheel to disaster

Crashing the SR/A1 fighter flying boat

The SR/A1 being towed to its mooring at Cowes, with Geoffrey Tyson in the cockpit.

The idea for a fighter flying boat arose in World War II from the paucity of airfields on the numerous small islands that were available to the Japanese in the Pacific theatre of war. Many of these islands had atolls which could provide operating bases for small flying boats, and so the Saunders-Roe company started work in response to official specification E.6/44.

The aircraft so conceived was the SR/A1, and was designed around two Metropolitan-Vickers F.2/4 Beryl turbojets. These were axial-flow engines, so two could be installed side-by-side in a reasonable hull width. The hull shape was of faired-V form and was entirely of metal construction, as was the rest of the aircraft.

Three prototypes of the SR/A1 were manufactured, with a slight variation in the maximum thrust produced by the engines. The first flight was made by Saunders-Roe chief

test pilot Geoffrey Tyson on 16 July 1947. The second prototype went to the Marine Aircraft Experimental Establishment at Felixstowe in 1948, and was lost with its pilot in poor visibility when he crashed into the sea while practising for an air display.

The third prototype, TG271, was magnificently displayed by Geoffrey Tyson at the 1948 Society of British Aircraft Constructors (SBAC) Show at Farnborough, with some superb inverted low

The SR/A1 was built to Ministry specification E.6/44, which aimed to create a seaborne fighter capable of operating in the tropics, where there were few airstrips. (RAF Museum Hendon P100522).

flying. This was the machine I was invited to fly in 1949, when commanding Aero Flight at RAE Farnborough

I flew down to Cowes in a Grumman Avenger on the morning of 12 August and had a briefing from Geoffrey Tyson. I then clambered aboard TG271, which was on beaching gear, and was gently eased down the slipway into the water. There the gear was removed and the aircraft was then towed by launch to the starting point, where both Beryls lit up first time without any trouble, so the tow was released.

I had already engaged the small water rudder, which was integral with the rear step in the hull and was linked to the rudder pedals, so followed the launch out into the Cowes Roads to the take-off position, finding the aircraft surprisingly easy to manoeuvre.

For take-off I decided not to use take-off flap, as this only improved the run time by two seconds and gave nose-up effect in unstick, due to the removal of the cushioning effect between the flap and water surface. Not having a lot of flying-boat experience, I found handling on take-off quite tricky, but had been well briefed by Geoffrey.

Once in the air I gave the aircraft a comprehensive work-out and found it had very acceptable flying characteristics with the possible exception of the stall.

Having completed my schedule of tests, I returned to base to prepare for landing. I was at 3,000 ft over Cowes when I received a radio call from the company launch that there had been a shift in the direction of the wind, thus necessitating reorientation of the landing lane, which would now need inspection by the launch to clear any floating debris. However, on reporting my fuel state it was realised there was

Above: An SR/A1 is towed to its take-off position.

Left: Saunders-Roe pilot Geoffrey Tyson and company designer Henry Knowler giving an interview on the day of the SR/A1's first demonstration flight, 30 July 1947.

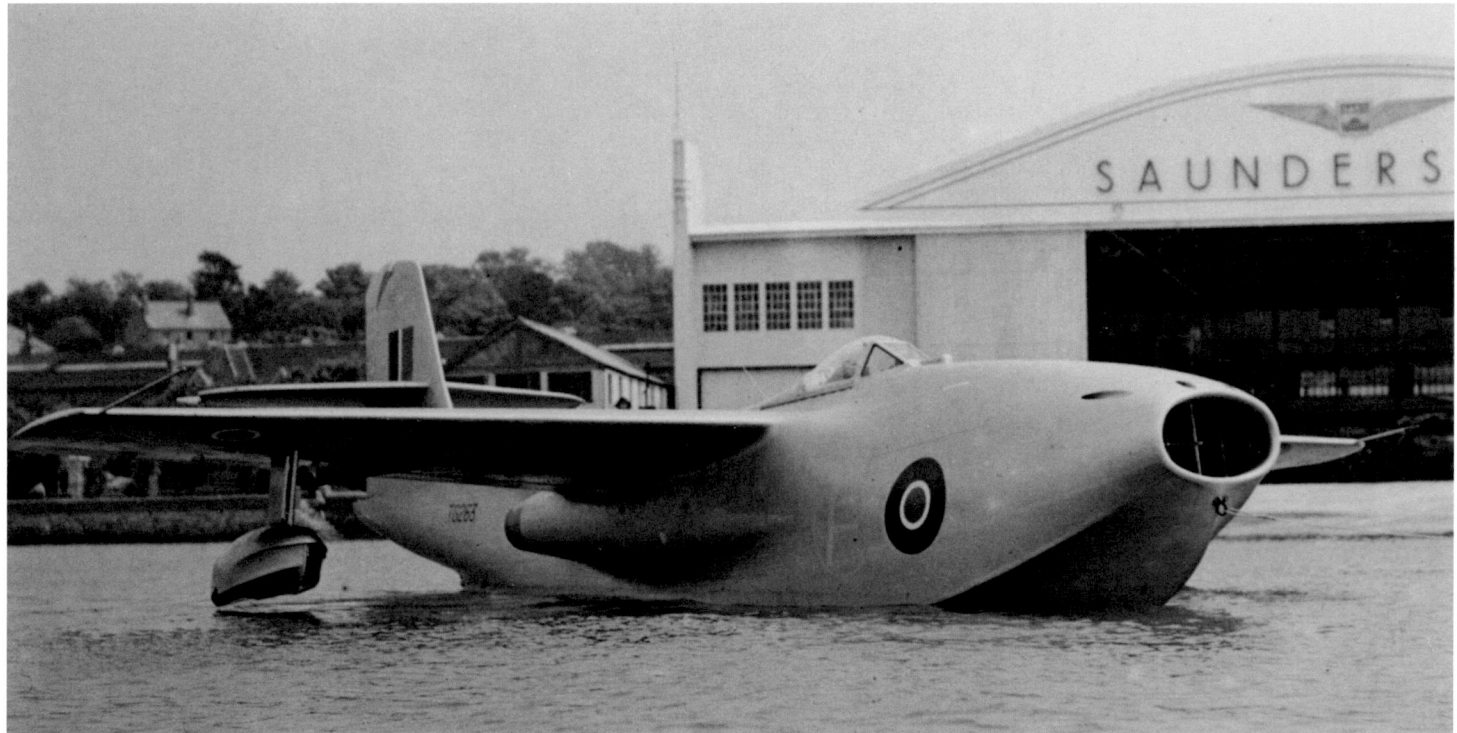

A promotional photograph of the SR/A1, TG263 in front of the Saunders-Roe factory at Cowes, Isle of Wight.

no time for the launch clearing procedure, so the risk of using an unswept lane had to be accepted, even though the wind was only about 5 mph and the water almost flat calm.

Anyway, the die was cast, and I eased the speed back to 150 mph at 1,000 ft and lowered the wing floats, followed by the flaps, and then opened the cockpit hood – a habit instilled in me from my experience in aircraft-carrier landings. I approached at 110 mph and held off slightly low so that the aircraft just kissed the water before settling on the deceleration run. At that moment I noticed a black object just protruding from the surface of the water dead ahead. There was a tremendous crash as the large piece of timber, probably from a dismasted yacht, struck the forebody planing bottom. Tearing a large hole in the hull it then shot out under compression and knocked the starboard float clean off the aircraft. The starboard wing dipped as the tip struck the water, then the aircraft cartwheeled and skidded along the surface completely inverted.

I was upside down in the cockpit and the water rushed past me at first, then started pouring in as the SR/A1 came to a halt. I undid my safety straps, hoping to fall out of the cockpit, but I was firmly held in by my unyielding parachute. Eventually I kicked free, having swallowed an enormous amount of water, and then found I could not surface because I kept hitting the top of the inverted wing.

Desperation is a great spur, and in spite of being half-drowned I got clear, but then felt myself losing consciousness before I could inflate my Mae West, so I did a 'dutch boy' act and stuck my finger firmly in a vent hole in the side of the hull. I was very obviously in poor shape at this point, but fortunately the company launch raced up and Geoffrey Tyson leapt fully

The SR/A1, TG263, on take-off runs during flight tests in Cowes Roads, Isle of Wight.

Michael Turner '14

Aug.	10	1510	1520	SELF	MR. TERNENT	HIGH SPEED TRACK ROCKET CRADLE - ARRESTER WIRE IMPACT PHOTOGRAPHY	S-51	VW 209
Aug.	11	1610	1700	SELF	4 CREW	SERVO TAB RUDDERS Followup ratio 0:1 Very touchy in response on take-off.	LANCASTER II	DS 708
Aug.	12	0940	1010	SELF	—	FLAPLESS GLIDE APPROACH AND LANDING PHOTOGRAPHIC HISTORY down to 115 mph	D.H. 108	TG 283
Aug.	12	1105	1125	SELF	—	FARNBOROUGH TO COWES.	AVENGER III	KE 446
Aug.	12	1440	1515	SELF	—	HANDLING. COMPRESSIBILITY DIVE TO M·82. Struck some driftwood's	SR/A.1	TG 271
						½ way along landing run. Aircraft slewed and turned turtle in 60' of water		
						in Cowes Roads.		

* AIRBORNE TIME ONLY, **NOT** TAXYING, TO BE SHOWN.

GRAND TOTAL [Cols. (1) to (8)]

3199 Hrs. 25 Mins.

Totals Carried Forward

'There was a tremendous crash as the large piece of timber, probably from a dismasted yacht, struck the forebody planing bottom …'

Jet fighter sinks

A Saunders-Roe flying boat jet fighter turned over and sank off Cowes, Isle of Wight, yesterday, while alighting after a test flight.

The pilot, Lieut.-Commander E. M. Brown, was rescued by launch.

·50							
·35							
5·35	26·45	4·55	591·10	·15	24·40 3·00	129·15	18·10	44·30
(3)	(4)	(5)	(6)	(7)	(8)	(9)	(10)	(11)

Having already carried out a photographically recorded flapless glide and approach on the infamous DH 108, Eric Brown flew straight to Cowes. Just over two hours later he took off on his ill-fated flight in the SR/A1.

Inserted in Eric Brown's log book; this rather brief account of his crash appeared in the Cowes local press.

Geoffrey Tyson flew the SR/A1 to London, landing on the Thames and mooring on the South Bank, as part of the Festival of Britain celebrations in 1951. (RAF Museum Hendon 6442-12)

clothed from it to my aid. I was taken to Cowes Hospital and overnighted there before flying myself back to Farnborough next day, none the worse for wear.

The observers in the launch reported that there were two holes in the forebody of the hull, one about four feet square, the other somewhat smaller. The aircraft sank as I was being hauled aboard the launch, and in spite of a continuing search up to the present day no trace of it has ever been found.

An overhead view of the SR/A1, showing its distinctive layout and unusually slender wings.

Index